AFTER THE WAR

AFTER THE WAR
IS OVER

Roger Lancaster

THE REAL PRESS
www.therealpress.co.uk

Published in 2021 by the Real Press.
www.therealpress.co.uk © Roger Lancaster

ISBN (print) 978-1912119134
ISBN (ebooks) 978-1912119127

For My Wee Rose

In loving memory of my early family – William,
Susannah, Iris, Robert and Clive.

Contents

Chapter one
Got any gum, chum?

I was born in February 1938, just over a year and a half before the start of World War II.

As Nazism rose rapidly in Germany during those 19 months, war became ever more inevitable to the British people. Furthermore, no-one thought we would ever be able to win it, except for a few crackpots like Winston Churchill, and even they must have been extremely doubtful behind all their fighting talk. Some people even committed suicide, feeling unable to face the humility of becoming enslaved and losing our country and empire.

My father told my mother during this time that he deeply regretted allowing them to produce a fourth child at such a time – I was the youngest of four and very much a late arrival, being eight years younger than my nearest sibling. My mother only told me this about half a century later. They could never have known then that I would go on to live a life which could hardly have been more happy, even from the start.

My father William was 45 when war broke out. He had served in the Great War more than twenty years before, thankfully in the Middle East mostly, so he was too old to be conscripted to this coming war. He had lost all his WW1 medals and always blamed my mother for letting their children play with them out in the pram and that they had been thrown out and lost during the 1920s and 30s. However, after my sister Iris died in 2018 and I had to deal with all her belongings, I found Dad's medals in a box – they had been there all the time.

My sister and two brothers, although being much older than me, were still too young to join up at the start. When the war began my sister Iris was 17, brother Robert, 13, and brother Clive, nine.

The first thing that I can ever remember was kneeling up in my pram, pushed by Iris, looking out at the traffic on the A435, which we called the "main road", through our village, halfway between Evesham and Birmingham. It was the beginning of a life-long interest in cars for me.

Our village was Coughton, pronounced Coe-Ton, and often erroneously pronounced Coffton. We lived in a 3-bedroom council house, one of six semi-detached houses halfway up a hill in Coughton Lane, a narrow road which joined the main A435 to the B4090, which was called the Droitwich Road and which led from Alcester through lovely villages and countryside to that town.

My maternal grandfather, Robert Butter, who was the gamekeeper, lived in the keeper's cottage with his second wife, my biological grandmother having died before I was born. The cottage was about half a mile further up Coughton Lane from our house and close to the Droitwich Road.

I can remember visits with my mother to Granddad's cottage, where he taught me how to tell the time, and where we spent a happy wartime Christmas. His job meant he had access to plenty of game and we could eat and drink well and played cards – a game called "tip it". But Granddad died in 1943 and the only Granny Butter I knew was moved down to live at a terraced cottage on the main road to make room for the new gamekeeper. I remember watching her being taken down past our house by a horse and cart, carrying all her belongings, which was quite sad.

The first thing I remember about the war itself happened one dark evening when my mother took me outside, followed by the rest of the family, to gaze into the night sky to see a bright red glow in the distance. It was the glow of the fires from the Coventry blitz, about twenty miles away. 500 German bombers raided the city for 11 hours, destroying the city, killing many hundreds and many more were injured, with others hysterical during the raid. There were other blitzes, of course, but Coventry caused the most anger, hatred and determination for revenge than any other. This was November 1940, when I was two years and nine months old.

Of course, I was too young during the early years of the war to understand anything much about it.

Coughton was largely immune from the bombing, the only two bombs dropped on our village fell on the cricket field – no doubt discarded by an enemy aircraft, the crew of which were anxious to get back home after being shot at over Coventry, Birmingham or Redditch.

Dad dug a big hole in our front garden and made a bomb shelter. It was tiny and the adults could not sit down upright inside it. I remember sitting in it just to try it out but it was never needed and I don't recall anyone else in the village making anything similar.

The German and Allied aircraft made quite different noises. Even the dogs knew it and were sensitive to our different reactions to the two sounds, barking when an enemy aircraft was overhead. We did not have a dog during the war but Granddad and some neighbours did.

As I was taken walks by Iris, I noticed that car headlights were mostly covered over to keep lights to a minimum at night, much of the traffic was military and some of the buses were temporarily driven by gas, with a gas balloon on top. Lorries had a number 20 painted on the back, indicating the maximum speed they were allowed. The largest vehicles of all were some enormous articulated Bedford lorries, each carrying two aircraft wings as they travelled southwards along the main road. We felt the wind from them as they passed by, which was quite often. Many years later I saw one of these lorries at the National War Museum at Duxford and was astonished by how small it looked then.

My mother joined the WVS (Women's Voluntary Service) and she was part of a group of women from the village who met in an old barn near the main road where they made camouflage nets for the Army. They were given plain netting with three-inch square holes together with strips of green and brown material. Their job was to thread the strips in and out through the netting in both directions to produce a very large camouflage net. Mum took me down there usually and I played around while the women worked and shared the local gossip. It was not every day, so I think they must have had several teams doing the job.

Iris had to give up her job working as a shorthand typist for Abel Morrall's needle factory in Redditch and do work for the war effort. I was later told that she was given a choice of three things she could do. She could join the army and become part of the ATS (Auxiliary Territorial Service, the women's part of the army) or become a Land Girl, working on the farm, or be a secretary for the Maudslay Motor Company, which made lorries. She felt she was not strong enough to work on the land and our parents forbade her to join the ATS, not because of any danger involved but because they thought the ATS had a bad reputation for leading young girls astray. So she began work at the Maudslay factory at Great Alne, about two miles away, again as a shorthand typist.

The Maudslay Motor Company was based in Coventry before the war but because of the danger from bombing, it was transferred to the tiny village of Great Alne, between Alcester and Warwick. The workers hated moving away from the town and having to live at the "back of beyond", as they saw it, even though it was much safer. Iris could either cycle through the country lanes, including crossing the River Arrow and passing through the farmland of Coughton Fields, or she could take one of the Black and White Company's coaches from a Harvington garage, which toured all the villages picking up people to work at the Maudslay. She would be in severe trouble if she was late getting to work and had to have a very good reason if she was ever sick, so she tended to go to work even when she felt very unwell.

Robert (Bob to his friends but always Rob to family) trained as a toolmaker and was desperate for the war to last long enough for him to join in the action. By the time he had been called up and completed his training, the war in Europe was over but the war against Japan was still going on. He had joined the Parachute Regiment and was on board the troopship *Corfu* on the way to Malaya when the war against Japan ended, so he was never involved in serious fighting. Clive was at school for most of the war but towards the end he worked for the Co-op, helping the driver deliver groceries from Alcester to all the surrounding villages.

We recycled paper and metal waste for the war effort by carrying it all down to a disused former blacksmith's shop at the junction of the main road and Wick Lane, which was a lane leading past the school and the railway station to the next village of Sambourne.

Wick was the name of an iron age fort, no longer noticeable, but it had been opposite where the railway station now was, and we usually called the lane Sambourne Lane.

Our next-door neighbours, Mr and Mrs Jordan had no children but they took in two evacuees from a less safe area of the country. They were two young sisters in their early or mid-teens. They were full of fun and once dressed me up in girls clothes and took me around the village to show me around, which I found rather embarrassing even though I was only about four. They were not there very long, being almost adults, but they kept in touch with the Jordans and we later heard that one of them had become a nun.

Mr Jordan had a car, a little Morris Eight, and he would drive to Redditch every weekday to work at the Royal Enfield motorcycle factory. When he returned from work he would often let me sit in his car while he opened his gate and drove into his drive. I would hang around for hours waiting for him to come home, hoping to get that little ride.

Across the road, in the garage of the Mildenhall's terraced cottage, there was another identical Morris Eight. It was out of use because its owner, the Mildenhall's son Joe, was being held as a prisoner of war in Crete. The Mildenhalls were devout Roman Catholics and prayed every night for his safe release, keeping a candle alight in their window all the time.

Mum took me on two holidays during the war while the others stayed at home working. Holidays for us always meant going to stay with one of our many relatives. The first was to Camerton Court, a stately home in Somerset, to visit my Auntie Doll, her husband Jack Reid and their daughter Joan. Uncle Jack was the gardener and Auntie Doll was the cook and housekeeper to the owner, Mrs Maconochie, a Jewish-American widow whose husband, who had been a civilian pilot, had died when his plane crashed while he was training a new pilot.

The main part of the large house was being used as a military hospital and both our relatives, their daughter Joan and Mrs Mac were living in the servants quarters. The Reids' rooms were above the garage and Mrs Mac lived on the same first upstairs floor nearby.

Mrs Mac had several cars, all of which I was allowed to play in. Two Buicks, one grey and the other black, together with a seven-seater Hudson Terraplane "woody" shooting brake (all of which were in storage in the stables) and a Morris Eight Series E convertible.

The only car in use was the Morris, which was dark red with black wings and always called the "little red car" and was used mostly by Uncle Jack and Joan.

Petrol was strictly limited but Jack was allowed petrol because he delivered vegetables from the gardens to local shops but he also used it for taking us out for rides, always careful to have a sack of potatoes in the back in case he was stopped.

There was a very large outbuilding which was about half the size of the main house and the military laundry formed a large part of it. Also, there was the generator which provided electricity for the whole Court, which Jack had to start just before sunset to provide lighting and stop it again in the morning – he often had great difficulty in starting it.

There were two army ambulances always parked in the drive at the front of the house, ready to leave at short notice, and I played in those as well. Often I would be visited there by an ATS girl, who was probably worried that I might cause damage or get hurt. There was much fun and laughter among the adults of our family and it was a wonderful holiday for me.

To get to Camerton we took the train from Coughton railway station, which was between Coughton and Sambourne, about a quarter of a mile from the main road. It stopped at every station and we had to change trains at Ashchurch. We had to wait at least two hours there, just sitting on a bench on the platform, then the next train took us to Radstock station, again stopping at every station on the way. From Radstock, we could have taken the bus, which ran from Frome to Bristol, with a stop at Camerton Court, but we would have had to wait up to an hour for the bus so Uncle Jack picked us up in the little red car. The whole journey took nearly all day but at least it could be done entirely by public transport, which would not be possible today. The journey by car today would take about two hours.

The other holiday was to London to visit my Mum's brother, Jack Butter, who lived alone in a tiny house near King's Cross station. The house had been built as an afterthought between two tall tenement buildings and was only wide enough for one small room at each of the three levels, the bathroom, toilet and kitchen being outbuildings behind.

Taking a holiday in London during wartime was a crazy thing to do, although it was later in the war and the worst of the blitz had passed.

Uncle Jack had been bombed out of two previous houses and I watched the searchlights operating through the bedroom window at night. Jack had a job at the Stationary Office which he loved, and he would leave us to ourselves during the day. He gave us a new Stationary Office dictionary. Such things were unobtainable normally at the time, but it was obviously a reject since a significant number of the pages were blank and inevitably any word we needed to look up would frequently be missing.

One day I saw a woman walking past and asked Jack if she was the Queen. Yes, she was, he assured me. He was always a bit of a joker. He had suffered mustard gas poisoning during the Great War in France, so he was never very well and never married.

While there one day we visited another of Mum's brothers, Uncle Maurice Butter, who was the landlord of the Red Lion pub at Thorpe, near Egham. He had a Citroen car stored in his garage which I was allowed to play in. We travelled there and back by Greenline bus.

I began my education at the local junior school in 1943. One day at school I did something terrible. I have never had any recollection of it but I was told about it by Iris some 60 years later. My cousin Ted Portman from Alcester was a pilot in the Fleet Air Arm and one day at school I told everybody that he had been killed when his plane had crashed. The word quickly spread and Ted's parents, my Auntie Nell and Uncle Howard heard it and were terribly distressed. They made inquiries and discovered that it was not true and that Ted was perfectly alright somewhere abroad. I had made it all up, probably wanting to gain some attention. However, a short time later they received the dreaded telegram that Ted had been killed when his plane crashed in, of all places, Canada. Ted's belongings were sent back to his parents but they were never told the circumstances of his death despite trying to find out for many years. I never knew Ted myself as he had joined up before I was old enough to know him but I did see a photo of him standing by his aircraft on his ship, which was always kept on the wall in his parents' front room.

Ted was a shortened name for anyone called Edward or Edwin. The trouble was that no-one knew which was the correct proper name - they would guess and often wrongly. My Dad's brother was a Ted and he was killed during the Great War in France, just three weeks before it ended, so Ted became an unlucky name for the Lancaster family and as far as I know, there has never been another since.

After school, we boys would wander slowly home and would sometimes see an army lorry carrying American GIs. We would shout out "Got any gum chum?" and they would usually throw us small packets of chewing gum. I did not like to chew gum very much but it was a fun thing to do.

I could never have dreamed then that one day my wife and I would have a lovely daughter who would marry a U.S. Army officer and that they would settle in Southam, Warwickshire, only a 40-minute drive from Coughton, and give us two wonderful grandchildren.

We children could play in nearby fields when not at school. We had nothing to play with so we would play war games, usually opening wide our arms pretending to be Spitfires or Messerschmitts, or play cowboys and Indians, imitating the western movies. Sometimes we would find a bright, wrinkled sheet of tin foil. I was told these were dropped by enemy bombers in an attempt to confuse our radar stations.

At home in the evening, we listened to the radio, mostly comedy shows, but sometimes we would tune in to listen to Lord Haw-Haw spouting German propaganda from Berlin. "Germany calling" he would say, then tell all the bad news about the war – Allied shipping sunk, etc. He would sometimes threaten to bomb Redditch, only six miles from Coughton, where there were many factories producing materials for the war effort. In particular, he said they would bomb the Big Hammer, which was a huge machine used to make parts for aircraft and we could hear its bangs in Coughton, but they did not hit it or as far as I know anything else in Redditch.

Around midday, a show called Workers' Playtime, for the benefit of those doing war work while they listened, was very popular, with songs and comedians like Gert and Daisy, Michael Hill and Benny Hill (not related as far as I know) and Nosmo King (it took me years to realise he had made up his name from a No Smoking sign). I still have that radio and it still works. It was bought new by Dad in 1934 after he had won a few pounds on the football pools.

One of the main topics of conversation during those times was about all the good things we could look forward to after the war was over. "After the war is over we will be able to buy bananas and chocolate", "After the war is over we will be able to tear down the blackout curtains and go outside at night with torches" (there was no street lighting in Coughton). "After the war is over we will be able to buy toys for your birthday and Christmas" and so on. There was a popular song, which was a huge hit in the late 1890s and which could still sometimes be heard on the radio. It was called "After the ball is over" and for years I thought they were singing "After the war is over".

Eventually, the war, in Europe at least, was over. On VE Day church bells rang out all over the country for the first time in years - Coughton parish church had a good team of bellringers. We heard of the celebrations on the radio and saw pictures in the newspapers, some of which published an edition in silver coloured paper.

Mum made a rag doll image of Hitler and hung it on a six-inch nail she hammered into the top of our front porch. We then got together with sticks and beat the doll until it was destroyed. Similar things went on all over the country, mostly in the form of Hitler images on bonfires as on Guy Fawkes night. Such hatred is hard to imagine these days and would probably be called a hate crime, but at that time the vast majority of people held such loathing of all Germans, Japanese and (to a lesser extent) Italians that no-one criticized the atomic bomb or the bombing of Dresden – it was cheered as vengeance for the blitz and the terrible atrocities committed in Hong Kong, Malaya, Burma and Singapore.

Sometimes I revisit Coughton and the last time I went, just a few years ago, that nail was still there on the front porch. Thankfully, for most people, such hatred did not last, even for those who had lost loved ones, and before long some whose families had not been personally affected by the war began to think we might have gone a bit too far with the bombing. In only a few years people began buying German and (a few years later) Japanese cars and goods. The Black and White garage at Harvington, whose coaches had taken Iris to work at the Maudslay, became a Volkswagen dealership and Iris and I bought a VW Beetle from them in the 1960s.

A few months after the war ended, Joe Mildenhall returned home from the POW camp in Crete. His parents' prayers had been answered and there was a great celebration in Coughton Lane when he arrived, with a large banner high over the road saying "Welcome home Joe". He would soon be driving his Morris Eight again and taking me to see motorcycle grass track racing at nearby Astwood Bank.

I had trouble with my throat and was always having to clear my throat. Some people, even the teachers, would be rather unkind, calling me piggy and so on. Mum took me to the wonderful Doctor Fitzmaurice at Studley about it and he said I should have my tonsils removed. This was standard practice at the time for anyone who had the slightest problem with their throat. So I had it done under anaesthetic at Redditch Hospital (then in the centre of the town). Afterwards, I was given my first ice cream for being a good boy.

The operation did nothing for me, however, and I still have to keep clearing my throat. Another treat was my first banana – these had been unavailable during the war. I was very disappointed with it - I had expected it to be juicy.

Chapter two
I will summon you

For centuries the village of Coughton centred around Coughton Court, the home of the Throckmorton family. At one time, practically everyone who lived in the village worked for or was somehow connected with the Court. My great-grandfather, William Lancaster, worked there as a wheelwright in the nineteenth century. All the farms in the area for miles around were owned by the Throckmortons and rented out to the farmers. Nearly all the cottages were owned by the Throckmortons, most being lived in by their employees, like my granddad, Butter, the gamekeeper who lived in the keeper's cottage near the top of Coughton Lane.

Right up until the early twentieth century the women who were employed as servants were not allowed to have male "callers" at the house and, as soon as they married, they had to leave. One of these was probably my great-grandmother Elizabeth Redding, who married William the wheelwright. There were practical reasons for this policy, for the women concerned as well as for their employers. With no appliances to help them, married women had a full-time job running a household and raising (often many) children and could not be expected to do a full-time job as well. Part-time jobs were not normally available in those days.

In my day the Court was the home of the Dowager Lady Throckmorton.

The A435 runs through the village from Evesham via Alcester then northwards towards Birmingham via Studley and is called the main road by the villagers. There is a crossroads, with Coughton Lane running west and Coughton Fields Lane running east, both narrow lanes. Coughton Lane leads up a hill and over what was then the railway line, ending up at a T-junction at the A422, called the Droitwich Road, between Alcester and Cookhill. Coughton Fields Lane leads to Great Alne village through Coughton Fields, which is a farming area, and the lane passes through the River Arrow at Coughton Ford. Cars drive through the ford and there is a narrow bridge for pedestrians and cyclists.

At the crossroads, opposite the former Post Office, there is an ancient monument, like a small square pyramid, enclosed by a tall iron fence, which is said to be a place where people who had passed through Feckenham Forest could pray for their safe deliverance, but there is no evidence to support this and the monument is something of a mystery. Just north of the crossroads, Sambourne Lane runs westward past the school (now the "old school") and the old railway station to the village of Sambourne.

The parish church, St. Peter's, is next to the Court and Lady Throckmorton had her own entrance door and pew behind the choir. There is a Roman Catholic church nearby off Coughton Fields Lane. The vicarage in my day was a grand house just off the main road, which had an orchard and gardens and a large lawn which was used for fetes. Adjoining it was the parson's pleck, a field between the vicarage and the Church of England school, which was across the road (Wyck Lane, or commonly called Sambourne Lane) and the field was used by the school for sports activities and games and used as an extra playground between lessons.

The River Arrow runs past the rear of the Court as it passes from Studley to Alcester and there is a smaller stream called Caine Brook, which flows from Sambourne into the Arrow, passing under a bridge on the main road at the bottom of the hill.

Between the vicarage and Caine Brook, there is a large house called Coughton House.

Lady Throckmorton was rarely seen in the village except passing by in her old Vauxhall limousine and driven by her chauffeur, Harry Wells, although she always visited the school for the annual sports day and presented the prizes. I only spoke with her once. She had asked me to visit the Court to mend her wireless set since she had heard that I did such things when I was about 14. I fixed it and she was very pleased, saying "If I need you again I will summon you." She never did, so I suppose the wireless gave no more trouble.

The only pub in the village is the Throckmorton Arms, halfway up the hill towards Studley. The landlord then was Thornton Swindon, who organised all the cricket matches and who occasionally took my Dad in his car to the horse races.

The cricket field was on the opposite side of the main road just north of Caine Brook and Thornton did very well when the cricketers retired to the pub after their match. Many of the visiting teams were from the Birmingham area and did not have a cricket ground of their own, one I can remember being Aston Villa Methodists.

Dad called at the pub nearly every night and Sunday mornings. Mum and Iris would go sometimes too and I would be left outside with other boys and brought some lemonade and Smiths crisps – there were seats in the porch of the main entrance door where we could wait, although we played in the car park and the field behind the pub when weather permitted.

Everyone in the village knew everyone else.

Len Parkes was an extremely busy man. His farmyard was behind the Post Office and corner shop (opposite the monument) which he ran nine to six. He was up very early baking bread and getting the milk from his farm ready for his van driver Harry Twentyman to carry around the village, together with the daily newspapers, in his old Ford eight van. Len was a bit of a joker and would tease the elderly women customers.

The letterbox was outside the shop and there was a telephone box nearby - we had no telephone at home so we used it for emergencies.

In the evenings Len would often work with the Studley Operatic Society and he was also busy in the Catholic Church. His farm contained an orchard and his biggest field ran from his farmyard up to the railway line and it was behind the hedge at the bottom of our garden. In the field, there were some lovely tall elm trees and a pit.

Another farmer was Mr Sumner, whose farm was at the opposite corner of the crossroads to the shop. His farm led from the river and then from the other side of the main road up to the railway line, on the opposite side of Coughton Lane to Len Parkes' field. Mr Sumner was not seen around much but we knew his two sons quite well.

Up Sambourne Lane, opposite the railway station, there was what was left of an iron age fort called Wyck, behind which was Cadbury's farm. The Cadburys were relatives of the Bournville chocolate people. Major Alan Cadbury had been in the Great War and kept his military title. All the family were very glamorous. The Major and Mrs Cadbury had four daughters – Sarah, Christina, Belinda and Amanda. Christina was about my age and was rather fiery at school but the other girls were more amenable.

Dad had been Major Cadbury's batman for a short time during the First World War and once worked at the farm for a while, looking after the horses and doing some gardening. He took me there once while he was working and I was allowed to play with a pedal racing car, a very splendid one with rubber tyres and modelled after the pre-war Mercedes Benz racing cars. I was also fascinated by a horse-drawn caravan they had in the yard.

The station master was Mr Ducket. Apart from the commuters to and from Redditch, the calls at Coughton station were very few and it was quite a shock for Mr Ducket on the few occasions we turned up in the middle of the day to catch a train, especially if we had bicycles with us. He was very dedicated to his work and if ever he was forced to travel by bus he would complain loudly if it was a minute late. The Duckets had a daughter and a younger son, Clifford, who was about 3 years older than me.

Billy Perkins was the church choirmaster and lived with his wife, daughter and younger son Peter, in a semi-detached cottage just downhill from the Throckmorton Arms. Billy tried hard to get all young people in the village to sing in the choir. Iris, Clive and Rob did so for a while but were not great singers, while I declined the offer, claiming tone-deafness. Billy had served in the Indian Army at one time and became well known for his stories beginning "When I was in Poona...." He was a staunch supporter of the Liberal Party at a time when hardly anyone else was. Peter was two or three years older than me.

Bert Deakin and his wife (I never knew the Christian names of any of the married women, they were all called Mrs something) and their daughter Jeanne lived in a semi-detached house near Caine Brook. They had once lived in the same group of council houses as us and were longtime friends of Mum and Dad. Jeanne grew up with Iris and they remained friends until Jeanne married and left the area. Bert had a good job at the Royal Enfield cycle and motorcycle works in Redditch and, also having only the one daughter, they were better off than us. They had once astonished the villagers by doing something previously unheard of in Coughton. They had a holiday abroad! To Ostende! Bert and Dad used to go on holidays together, fishing at Mordiford, near Hereford, both travelling there on Bert's tiny Royal Enfield 125cc motorcycle.

We lived in the middle one of the three semi-detached council houses up Coughton Lane, between the main road and the railway bridge. Our next-door neighbours were the Jordans who had no children. In the two houses below us were the Smiths and the Boots, neither of whom had children. Both couples were retired and Mrs Boot did a lot for the church. In the two houses above us were Harry Mason with his wife and children Des (Desmond) and Kit (Kathleen) and an ugly black dog called N****r. (No-one thought there was anything wrong with the dog's name – people living in rural Warwickshire in those days never saw a black person).

Des was with the army in India for a while and after his return he became the nearest thing to a politician in Coughton, being chairman of Coughton Parish Council. Next to the Masons were the Goddards and their son Lionel. Edgar Goddard had an unusual job delivering steam rollers from Bomford and Evershed's factory in Evesham to places all over the country, driving the steam rollers and towing a caravan in which he could sleep at night because his journeys took so long.

Lionel was about the same age as Iris and was a very enthusiastic railway engine driver. There were three families called Goddard in Coughton but I don't think any of them were related.

Across the road from us was a pair of semi-detached cottages, the toilets of which were a long way away down their gardens. (Our council houses had outdoor toilets but they were very close to our back doors). In one of these cottages were the Mildenhalls with their son Joe, who was slightly older than Iris, and in the other were the Goodenoughs and their daughter (or possibly granddaughter) Jean, who was my age. The Goodenoughs, Smiths and Masons were all slightly related but I never knew how exactly.

There were a few thatched cottages in Coughton Lane between our house and the main road. A pair of elderly spinsters lived in adjacent ones and a widow and a widower, both elderly, lived in semi-detached ones opposite. The widower was a Mr Partridge, whose son was the Bishop of Nandyal in central India. The bishop's name was Arthur and he did not come home much but I did meet him aboard ship once in 1958 when he was travelling back to the UK on a rare visit. Later, Mr Partridge and his neighbour were married in their old age. There was also a group of tiny almshouses for the poor at the bottom of the lane, adjoining the main road and very close to it. These houses were occupied by elderly widows and the noise from the traffic on the main road must have been deafening for them (there being no such thing as double glazing).

After the war, a pair of wooden semi-detached houses were built between our houses and the railway line. They were called Swedish houses and were quite substantial. Also, four more council houses were built downhill from our group.

After my Granddad died in 1943, my Gran moved to a cottage on the main road, between the Post Office and Sambourne Lane, where she lived with her daughter from her first marriage and her daughter's son Harry Bridges, who was about the same age as Clive. Harry was well educated and had a good job at the Entaco needle factory in Studley, which later became Needle Industries.

For a while, following a request from the church, Gran took in a man from the Birmingham area who was paralysed, only able to stay in bed all the time, and I would sometimes visit him and chat to him, which he seemed to like, but he died when I was still quite young.

Chapter three
You'll get like your Uncle Maurice

During the war and for some years after there was, of course, food rationing. Clothing was also rationed. There were things which were not rationed but they were often difficult to obtain because most production and materials had to be for the war effort.

The Lancaster family knew all about going without. My Dad was born and brought up in a two-bedroom house, divided from the adjoining house by an entry, in Littlewood Green, part of the large village of Studley, two miles north of Coughton. In the 1901 census, there were three William Lancasters living in that house – my Dad, who was seven, his father and his grandfather. All firstborn sons of the Lancaster family were called William from as far back as I can tell.

Also living there was my grandmother, Betsy Anne (who we called Granny Lanc), Dad's siblings and two of his uncles. There was no room for Dad's oldest sister Nelly, who lived with her uncle a few houses away.

Dad's childhood was one of desperate poverty. His father and two uncles were the only sources of income for the whole family so they had to be fed reasonably well, which meant that Dad could only eat any food they left. Dad told us that his mother would sometimes make a "hayrick" for him to eat. This was made by filling a cup with stale bread and pouring tea, complete with tea leaves, over it, then tipping it all out of the cup upside down, the result looking like a hayrick. The only toy he ever had, he told us, was a cardboard crocodile. He had to attend the nearest school, even though it was one of a different church denomination to the Lancasters, to save on shoe leather. He attended three different Sunday schools of various denominations so that he could go on all their free days out each year – the only chance he had to go anywhere.

Dad had a phobia about OHMS. Official government letters always came in brown envelopes with the words "On His (or Her) Majesty's Service" and as soon as one arrived at our house Dad would throw it into the fire without opening it. It might have been a cheque for all he knew but he would never look at it, assuming it was bad news asking for the little money he had.

My Mum's family, the Butters, were better off, mainly because most managed to find jobs which included the use of a house. In the past most had been gamekeepers like my Granddad and my Uncle Frank, who lived in keepers' cottages, but two uncles (Len and Bob) had good jobs in the Welsh Forestry Commission, Maurice had the Red Lion and Doll was at Camerton Court. Jack had to rent a house in London but he was single so had few commitments and he had a steady job.

My Uncle Jim (actual name Henry Arthur Butter) had disappeared shortly after the Great War and was generally thought to have run away from his wife and son. He was never seen or heard of again by any member of the family, much to the distress of his parents. Even worse for my grandparents, their daughter Ada Florence Butter died from drowning in the well over the road from their keeper's cottage at Coughton in 1927 and my grandmother died the following year – my Mum said from a broken heart. My Granddad later married Ada Summers, who had been the landlady of the Green Dragon pub at Sambourne, and she was the Gran I knew.

Not one of our wider families had ever been able to buy their own home, although Uncle Len built one for himself in Bwlch, South Wales, and Maurice might have been able to buy one late in his life after leaving the Red Lion but I am not sure.

Before the war, Dad, who by skill was a maker of fishing rods, had been able to earn enough to have a second-hand car. One was a Calthorpe, bought from the headmaster of Alcester Grammar School, and the later one was a Standard called "Redwings" for obvious reasons. I never knew these since the costs of keeping three children must have made cars too expensive to run before I arrived.

The fishing rod industry suffered many ups and downs and so Dad often had to work in other factories and for a while looked after the horses and gardens of the Cadbury farm in Coughton. To make ends meet he would also cycle around the villages selling clothing, mostly paid for at a shilling a week.

The clothing came from the Bell and Nicholson wholesale store in Birmingham, in which Mum had an account, which she was able to get via my Auntie Flo (Dad's sister) who was in partnership with another lady, a Mrs Jones, who had a small shop selling sweets and clothing in Studley. All our clothing came from Bell and Nicholson as well, as did sweets which Mum could sell in our village, although the rationing stopped that. My clothes were all "bought to allow for growing" so they were all too large most of the time.

Mum, like most housewives at the time, had no work-saving appliances so had far too much work to do in the home to allow her to have a full-time job, but she made some money by making fishing tackle at home and selling it to a shopkeeper from Coventry. Both my parents worked extremely hard to provide for us all.

We did have three luxuries: the radio, a piano and a gramophone. The radio was an Ultra, bought in 1934, and was used constantly by Mum throughout the day and we all enjoyed the evening entertainment provided. The piano was very old, an upright with movable candlesticks above the right and left sides. It worked quite well though and Iris had learned to play from music to a very limited extent. I managed to play a few tunes on it by ear when I was in my early teens.

I also took piano lessons for a couple of years from Miss Jarrett of Studley but I did not study the things she gave me, preferring to play popular songs by ear. (She did take me to Birmingham where I passed the Primary Grade of the Royal Schools of Music in 1949).

The gramophone was also old - we had only a few pre-war records and finally, the spring broke. Both the piano and the gramophone were around long before I was born and had probably either been given to us or bought second hand before the war.

The rationing was extremely severe – for example just one egg per person per week. Ration books contained coupons for buying all the different types of food. We could add to it by keeping chickens in a large coop at the bottom of the garden with a big outdoor netted space for them to run around. This gave us eggs and a chicken dinner for Christmas and Easter but because of it, we were not allowed coupons for eggs.

Some people kept a pig in a sty in their back gardens and they were not allowed coupons for bacon or ham.

Mum fed the chickens with a mixture of stale bread, potato peelings, water and some kind of corn powder which you could buy to add to it and mix it all up. Mum also raised chicks in a small coop on the front lawn. They were lovely when young but sometimes one would be born sickly and Mum would bring it into the house and put it in an old handbag near the fire, trying to make it eat and drink, but they usually died anyway.

When we had a chicken for a meal, Dad would kill it by breaking its neck and Mum would feather it out in the coal shed before de-gutting it in the kitchen. No-one else in our family would kill a chicken and one time Dad was sick in bed when we wanted one killed, so Rob caught it and took it upstairs to the bedroom where Dad had to sit up in his sickbed to do the job.

Our house had a huge back garden and Dad made really good use of it, harvesting enough vegetables to last the whole year and we rarely had to buy vegetables. He really "dug for victory", as the official wartime sign prompted us to do, and he carried on doing it after rationing for as long as he was able.

Another thing we could get were rabbits, at first from Granddad and later from one of the farmer's boys. Mum made great rabbit stews and pies. Another favourite was made from a small tin of salmon mashed up with enough peas, mashed potatoes and parsley sauce to make a meal for six. One treat we could get occasionally was a small tin of crab meat from Russia, which I guess must have come aboard ships of the Arctic convoys returning from Murmansk.

Rob had a pen pal in New Zealand, a girl called Daphne, whose family sent us occasional parcels packed with food we could otherwise only dream of. Some years after the war we were able to send toy cars, Dinky Toys, to Daphne's son when they were not able to get them in New Zealand. Also, I was able to visit the family and thank them personally when my ship visited Wellington in 1959.

For breakfast, we would usually have bread and milk or porridge. We had only one full meal a day – in the evening on weekdays (which we called tea) and around midday on Sundays (which we called dinner). Lunch to us meant sandwiches for midday meals at work or school and these were very strange: apple sandwiches, tomato ketchup or Daddies sauce sandwiches, others of Marmite, brown sugar or beetroot in season.

Heinz sandwich spread and Lyle golden syrup were good when we could get them. Tinned meat was Spam, which no-one liked in our house, but the stewed steak was good – one tin to feed a family of six. People longed for old fashioned white bread – I thought the bread we had was white anyway, knowing none different, but it was more grey.

My family were all great tea drinkers. "A nice cup of tea" was a remedy for anything and copious cuppas were swallowed several times every day. I could not stand tea myself, even the smell of it made me feel sick, but I drank it in the belief that if I did not I would die, but as soon as I discovered that it was not a necessity to human life I stopped drinking it and have never done so since.

The Co-op delivered groceries once a week. Local farmer, baker and shop owner Len Parkes sent a van around every day delivering newspapers, bread and milk. The milk came in a bucket and the driver had a pint jug which he used to measure the amount before pouring it into our jug. Butcher Reg Grummet from Alcester delivered meat once a week and Fosters from Studley sent a mobile ironmongers-shop along once a week, from which we could buy paraffin, soap and matches and which carried lots of other things which we could not afford. If one of our saucepans had a hole in it Dad could buy a special gadget with a rubber seal which he could screw into the hole to seal it up. A new saucepan would have been far too extravagant.

Everyone had to very careful how much they ate at every meal. At Sunday dinnertime Dad would chastise us if we started by eating the meat – we were supposed to fill up with the vegetables first. Also, he urged us to "lean over" the table so that we did not waste any food by dropping anything onto the floor. If any of us wanted anything special to eat we would be accused of being "nice hungry". Any member of the family who tried to steal an extra bit of any food would be threatened with the warning "You'll get like your Uncle Maurice!" To see a fat person anywhere was very rare during rationing but Uncle Maurice was an exception, being rather portly.

One morning Mum made a pie in a thin circular tin plate from a can of stewed steak from our rations, which had to serve a family of six, putting it in the safe in the pantry (no-one we knew had a fridge then) ready for the evening tea. Then she went off to Birmingham shopping (there was a 148 Midland Red bus every hour between Evesham and Birmingham and the two buses going each way passed Coughton at the same time).

My friend David Atkins and me were playing at our house after school and we were hungry, as we always were. I cut a couple of small pieces of the pie for us to eat. That made us hungry for more so we had another couple of pieces. Soon the whole pie had gone – it was not very much. When Mum came home and saw what we had done she was furious and the whole family had to go without a proper meal. Fortunately, before long everyone saw the funny side of it - it was laughed about for years and was never forgotten.

Petrol, clothes and furniture were also rationed. The government introduced utility clothing and furniture, which were produced using very basic materials by industry to provide good, cheap items. These had a logo printed on the inside which was meant to read CC41, although the Cs looked like three-quarter black circles and the 1 was much bigger than the 4. For many years after the war, we were still wearing clothes with the utility sign on.

Our council house was a very cold place in the winter. Granny Lanc called it "starve hall". We had a coal fireplace in the front room, which was our living room, and a "Fairy" cooking range in the kitchen which was also coal-fired. They were our only sources of heat in the house normally. Coal was delivered in bags by the coalman who emptied them onto the floor in the coal shed, from where we had to collect it as required.

We had an electric fire but it was too expensive on electricity to use unless there was a dire emergency. The doors and windows all let cold air in and we covered them with curtains and "sausage cushions" at the base of the doors but these were not very effective. We all often suffered chilblains by putting our freezing feet too near the fire after coming in from the cold. Piped gas was never possible in Coughton.

Our toilet was outside and in the winter Dad would light a paraffin heater in it. For night time use we had chamber pots underneath each bed. We did not have an inside toilet until the 1970s – the council officer who collected our rent every week told Mum that the Coughton houses were called the "odds-and-sods" at the council offices and were the last in the county to get any improvements.

Each morning Mum spent hours fetching water in buckets from the pump in the front garden, clearing the fires and relighting them, emptying the potties, doing the washing, and house cleaning. She always did all the decorating, which was basic painting – we had no wallpaper. The ceilings were white but were soon turned brown because Mum, Dad and Iris all smoked continually. All the woodwork was painted with Darkaline, which was dark brown and the whole interior of the house was very drab.

Mains electricity had been possible since before the war because Coughton Court paid for having it connected to them and they made it available to everyone in the village who wanted it. Most accepted it but the Jordans next door would not have it and used paraffin heating and lighting instead.

We did not have tap water until after the war. There was a pump between our house and the Jordans, connected to a well, and we (usually Mum) had to carry water in buckets from the pump to the kitchen, next to which was a tiny bathroom with bath and sink, and to the outside toilet for flushing. The bath had a mangle on top, which covered half of the bath, for part drying the laundry, after which it had to be dried on the line outside in the garden. For laundry washing, in the kitchen, there was a "copper", which was a large permanent bricked-in metal bowl for the water and this was coal-fired from underneath.

After the war, Mum saved up sixty pounds over a period of years to have the Fairy range changed for a Rayburn, which was a smaller version of the Aga cookers and used coke. This also heated the water, so we had hot and cold water on tap for the first time in the 1950s, by which time our house had been connected to main water pipes.

Toys were virtually impossible to obtain during the war but I had some pre-war Dinky toys to play with. They were given to me by the Caile family, who lived in an idyllic cottage deep in the fields along the Droitwich Road.

Mrs Caile was a great friend of Mum's and they often worked together making fishing tackle and chatting away while doing so. Mr Caile had died years before and his wife had married a Mr Chambers but poor Mr Chambers' status was never recognised by Mum and she remained Mrs Caile to us. She had two sons – Philip, who was about Rob's age, and Geoffrey, who was about Clive's age, and Clive and Geoff were great friends.

The two boys had outgrown Dinky toys so they were passed on to me. They were all pre-war of course and my favourite was a Lagonda, others I remember being an Armstrong Siddeley, a Frazer Nash, a Packard and a Scammel lorry. The Cailes also had a Hornby train set, which they kept, but I was allowed to play with it whenever I went to their house with Mum. I played for hours with the toy cars, outside when it was warm daylight, inside when cold or dark. Playing down on the floor with the cars indoors made it easier for me to breathe because the smoke tended to rise away from the floor.

An elderly lady lived in the adjoining cottage to Mrs Caile – she was either Mrs Caile's or her husband's mother. I can remember when I was still a toddler this lady had me into her house sometimes where she sat me on her table with bowls and jugs of water which I could play with, pouring water around from one to another, which I quite enjoyed doing.

I remember one Christmas receiving seven draught boards from various aunts and uncles, but only one set of draughts made from recycled paper.

One year some Italian prisoners of war held nearby made some wooden toys for local children. Some prisoners were allowed to work on nearby farms during daylight hours, although I never saw one. I was given a wooden toy from them which was like a table tennis bat with three chickens on the top, their movable heads connected via string to a wooden weight underneath. When you swung the bat around, the chickens' beaks would tap on the bat in sequence. It was very clever but became rather boring after a few minutes.

Whenever we moaned about lack of food or lack of toys for me, Dad would always tell us we were lucky and forever repeat that when he was young he had to eat hayricks and his only toy was a cardboard crocodile.

One day, Rob and Iris made a hayrick just as Dad had said it was made and gave it to him for his tea. We all had a good laugh, except Dad who would not touch it.

After the war rationing continued, only gradually ending bit by bit until meat rationing finally ended in 1954.

Dad returned to making fishing rods at a small business in Redditch, cycling six miles there and six miles back every weekday. It did not pay much (he never earned as much as ten pounds a week) but he also made rods in our garage in the evenings and at weekends, selling them to anglers who visited the Throckmorton Arms. Mum continued making fishing tackle.

Rob was away in the Far East, serving in the Parachute Regiment. Clive had a girlfriend, Kathleen Laight in Cookhill and they married when they were very young – he did his National Service after working for the Co-op and afterwards drove a van for the Redditch Laundry company – so the main breadwinner of our remaining family became Iris and she had obtained a good job as a secretary in a solicitor's office in Redditch.

Toys slowly became available again. Iris found that a Redditch garage occasionally had new Dinky Toys for sale and she snapped up some during her lunch breaks for me whenever possible. Christmas and birthday presents for me included a John Bull printing outfit, a Meccano-style set called Trix, moulds for making farm animals from scrap lead (mostly from finished toothpaste tubes) and a train set (not a Hornby, just a very simple one). But I was becoming too old for some of these things. I enjoyed using Iris's old Remington typewriter and I became quite adept in its use, which served me well when I went off to sea as a radio officer years later.

Very gradually we were able to buy more things to make life a little easier. We paid for the gramophone clockwork mechanism to be sent to Garrards, the manufacturers, to be repaired, which took many weeks by post. Mum bought a spin drier, Dad a lathe for his work in the garage. Rob and Clive bought old second-hand motorbikes and later cars. Iris bought a dog which she liked to take for walks around the countryside.

I longed for a bicycle and Dad promised to get me one from Bert Deakin who worked at the Royal Enfield works in Redditch and could get them at a lower price. I waited years for that bike and when it did come it was "bought to allow for growing" and was much too big for me. I had to have a different seat strapped to the crossbar, bits of wood put on the pedals and I could only get going on it by standing it next to a bank or kerb, but I was mobile at last.

Later, when Rob was married to Brenda, they lived in Studley and had a baby boy, Brett, and Rob decided to change his motorbike to one with a sidecar. It was an old 650cc Norton and the sidecar had two seats, one behind the other. He brought it back to Coughton for us to see and took us up the road for a ride in it.

I was behind him on the pillion seat and Brenda was in the sidecar with Brett. Rob was demonstrating to us that, because of the sidecar, he had to rev up when turning left and brake when turning right when he suddenly lost control and we bounced across the grass and into a ditch beneath a thorn hedge. I was hurled over Rob and into the hedge while Brenda and Brett were pushed right into the front of the sidecar. None of us seemed to be hurt so we set off back home and decided not to tell Mum or Dad about it. Back home, however, Mum suddenly stared at me and cried "What have you done to your face?" The scratches from the thorn bush had begun to bleed.

By the mid-1950s we could afford to use our electric fire and were given a small secondhand electric "Baby Belling" cooker. We had to wait even later for a fridge and a TV set.

In the mid-1950s Coughton Parish Council tried to bring street lighting to the village. It took them years to get it organized then they had to get the villagers to vote for or against it. All was going well until word got around that it would cost everyone an increase in their housing rates duty, then it was voted against, so it never arrived.

Mum wanted to buy and set up a light on the outside wall of our house as a "friendly light" for passers-by, but she wanted it to be red. Even I was old enough by then to know that a red light outside our house at night would not be a good idea. Mum could not understand why we were all so against it. There was no way we would allow it but none of us could bring ourselves to explain to Mum why.

Uncle Maurice died at Coughton on a rare visit to stay with us for a few days. He suffered from angina and had just walked up the hill from the shop. He sat down in an armchair in the front room to have a cup of tea and he suddenly passed away quite peacefully.

Chapter four
Cats in the artist's studio

In 1943, I was old enough to start school. Coughton Church of England school was in Sambourne Lane, a short walk from the main road (it has now been replaced by a new school in Coughton Lane). The school had a good reputation and served Sambourne as well as Coughton. Some people from Alcester and Studley also sent their children there, rather than their local schools. There were only two classrooms – a small one for the young ones, taught by Miss Yapp from Studley, and a big room for the others, taught by the headteacher, Mrs Moizer from Alcester. Children were there up until the age of 15 unless they passed the 11 plus and went to Alcester Grammar School, so the big room was divided into groups of different ages but all taught by one person, Mrs Moizer – although occasionally a young helper would join her briefly for training.

Both teachers were excellent and I remember Miss Yapp having great difficulty in making me pronounce the word "said" properly. I always pronounced it "sayed" instead of "sed" but my family were astonished one day when they discovered I could read at a very early age. They asked me to read from the local newspaper, the Redditch Indicator, and I could read everything, even the financial page, without even knowing what it was about. I don't think I was exceptional, all the other pupils started reading early as well. Miss Yapp was very popular with her pupils as she made every lesson interesting and sometimes fun.

We were given a small glass of milk mid-way through the morning. For lunch, we had sandwiches, although after the war cooked meals were brought by van for lunch from a place near Birmingham. The meals were in steel containers and they must have kept the food very hot for a long time as I'm fairly sure they did not need re-heating. I don't think my parents had to pay for the meals. We kids were not fussy about food, having lived so frugally for so long, except when it came to rice pudding when there would be choices to be made as to who wanted skin and, if so, who wanted black skin and who wanted yellow skin.

The playground was divided equally between boys and girls, only accessible across the path to the main entrance of the building, which no-one had any desire to cross.

Outdoor toilets were provided for boys and girls in their separate areas. A pump for water was in the boy's playground. The village cemetery was behind a wall next to the girl's playground and while I was there a new wooden cycle shed was built in the girl's playground. Across the road were steps leading up a steep bank to a gate into the playing field, the parson's pleck. This steep bank was also used as a rockery garden where pupils could learn bits of gardening, each of us being given a tiny area to work on.

Mrs Moizer was a good teacher and she had a good reputation for getting pupils to pass the 11-plus, hence the popularity of the school for miles around.

Pupils sat at desks for two which had space beneath for books and there were also inkwells for each pupil. There were two coal fires at the wall behind the teacher's chair and the pupils' desks were on the other side away from the fires, so we could be cold in winter. Blackboards and easels were the only visual aids, although there was a rather grand console wireless receiver, the only thing I can remember it being used for was to listen to "Music and Movement" from the BBC, to which we had to do physical exercises in time with the music.

We boys could occasionally get up to some mischief during playtime. During heavy rain, the older boys would sometimes block up the drain in the road and cause a big flood all over Sambourne Lane. Once one boy brought along some live gun bullets and we tried to set them off by dropping bricks on them, but fortunately we were not able to. Another time some of us were caught "scrumping" - stealing apples from the vicar's orchard – and I had the cane for that (the only time). There was very little fighting during playtime but I often fell, always on my knees, so I frequently went home with blood on my knees and sometimes the teacher would put iodine on them, which would sting quite badly.

After I had been at school for a year Mum decided it was time for me to start going to Sunday school so she sent me off on my own one Sunday morning. I assumed that Sunday school would be held at the school so that's where I went. No-one else turned up and I saw some of the older pupils ride past the school on their bicycles, which I thought rather odd. It did not occur to me that Sunday school would be held at the church so I went home and told Mum no-one else had turned up. Mum did not know I had gone to the school and thought I just didn't want to go to Sunday school, so she gave up the idea for another year.

By the time I did go to Sunday school we had a new vicar, the Reverend Harrison, and his wife held the Sunday school in the sitting room of their vicarage. The previous vicar had not been popular but the Harrisons were a very nice couple. They had come to us from Shottery, which was part of Stratford-upon-Avon, and they had loved it there, so they regretted moving to Coughton. However, they made the best of it and their fetes were very popular.

Mrs Harrison gave us a stamp of a Bible scene for each time we visited Sunday school and after her lesson, we had to draw a picture of the story but we were never allowed to include a drawing of Jesus in it – instead, we had to draw a cross in place of Jesus. She had us performing a Nativity play each Christmas and around Christmas time each year they took us by coach to the theatre at Stratford to see "Toad of Toad Hall". It was always "Toad of Toad Hall".

One year I had forgotten all about the outing and had gone off with the laundryman on his rounds around the villages in his van, which I sometimes did. The coach was held up while they searched for me but could not find me so they had to go without me. I was not very popular but I was not too sorry either since by now I was totally fed up with "Toad of Toad Hall" and thought it was very silly.

I learned a lot of swear words at school, which caused severe embarrassment to my parents when I came out with them at home and in company, which I often did. Mum threatened me, saying I would be sent to the "Swear House" if I kept doing it. She blamed Harry Mason for teaching them to me, but I cannot remember him doing so – I thought I had learned it all at school. One day I was walking through Alcester with Mum when we passed by the Town Hall, which is an ancient gaunt-looking building, and I asked Mum if it was the Swear House. "Yes it is!" she replied, "and that's where you'll be sent if you keep swearing." I cannot remember whether that did the trick or not but I finally managed to contain my enthusiasm for the habit.

Mrs Moizer was strict but fair. One day Rob came home from the army having returned from abroad, which could have been Palestine or Malaya, I cannot remember. He cheekily came into the school and asked Mrs Moizer if he could take me out of school for an hour to talk with me and, surprisingly, she agreed. We walked into the playing field and chatted for an hour.

One really nasty episode took place one day. Owners of pets and small working animals did not use vets very much in those days. My granddad had to shoot his dogs when they became too old to work efficiently, which really upset him because he had grown fond of them and the dog knew what was going to happen beforehand.

Alongside the boys' playground, was Len Parkes' farmyard and this morning one of his labourers chose to shoot one of the dogs. We heard the bang of the first shot which was followed by screams from the dog. Then there was another shot and more screams. The man had made a mess of the business and the poor dog howled for what seemed a very long time before a final shot ended it. Mrs Moizer ran out of the room and went across to the man to give him a severe piece of her mind because we children were very upset by it.

I don't remember much about our lessons but one book sticks in my mind. It was called "Tales of an Old Yew Tree" and told history lessons about things that had happened under a yew tree over the years. I thought it was a very clever idea but I cannot remember any of the stories. I did OK in the English and maths except for the problem pages of one of the maths books. They were way beyond my means. They would read something like: "If I buy 13 pounds of potatoes at twopence farthing a pound, a quart and a half of milk at sixpence halfpenny a pint, four ounces of wheat at two shillings and sixpence a bushel and three and two-thirds pounds of beetroot at a penny-farthing an ounce, how much change would I receive from two guineas?"

In the spring of 1947, the whole country was snowed under for about six weeks. The school remained open but only seven of us could normally make it over that period. Most of the children from outside the village could not walk through the deep snow, although the teachers made it and must have walked to and from Alcester and Studley every day unless they had found somewhere to stay during the week.

Only tractors and heavy lorries had any chance to move anywhere and only then along major roads where some of the snow had been piled at the sides. Clive worked on the Co-op grocery van with driver Les Fowler and they managed to do all their deliveries to all the villages but they had to carry the produce in sacks on foot much of the way.

The teachers did not think it worthwhile to teach normal lessons and I expect they thought the snow would soon disappear so they let the seven of us who could get there gather around the fire all day and gave us some paper on which to draw pictures. I had no imagination in the art field and could only draw pictures of vans, lorries and planes, so it all became very boring for us all and we chatted together most of the time.

As we approached the time for the 11 plus we had to do a lot of problem-solving of what were called intelligence questions, which were part of the exam. They could be very bewildering too. One I remember was "An artist had two cats, one fully grown and one small kitten. So that he would not be interrupted by the cats wanting to enter and leave his studio, the artist cut

47

two holes in the door – a large hole for the cat and a small hole for the kitten. Why was this silly?" Many suggestions were made, such as both cats could use one large hole, how would the kitten know the difference? They could leave the door open all the time, he could shut them out of the house, and many more. None of them, however, was the right answer. I never did find out what the right answer was and am still wondering about it now. One famous question became well known. It was "Which is the odd one out between a dog, a cat and a wireless set?" Most of us chose the wireless set because the others were animals, but that was not the right answer. The answer required was the cat because both the dog and the wireless set required a licence to be paid for by the owner (in those days), but cat owners did not need a licence.

The examination itself was held in the small room, invigilated by Mrs Moizer. I pretended not to care about whether I passed or not, on the basis that a pessimist can never be disappointed, but I really wanted to pass and go to the Grammar School of course. In the English section, we had to write a story about any dream we had had before the exam. I made up a weird story about being attacked by doctors in white coats who were trying to inject me. Mrs Moizer seemed quite pleased with my effort when she read what I had written but she could not make any comments.

I did pass the exam and would be going to the Grammar School in Alcester in September 1949. All my family were delighted since no-one in our immediate family had been to the Grammar School before. Iris had passed the exam but in her day she had to go to the school for an interview and she was rejected – Dad was convinced that it was because they had asked her what her father did for a living and she had to tell them he worked in a factory.

Dad gave me a wristwatch as a present for winning. Watches were very expensive in those days and I had never worn one before.

In preparation for my future schooling, I decided to buy a set of ten encyclopedias – the New Universal Encyclopedia – and paid for them monthly at one pound a month from my pocket money which I received from Iris. Mr Ducket had to deliver the books from the railway station on his bicycle and he said they weighed forty pounds. Halfway through the payments, Dad paid the remaining money.

I took those books with me to sea and when I emigrated to New Zealand, then brought them back again and I still have them. They remained useful for many years provided the information required was pre-1947, although they have now finally become obsolete thanks to Google.

Chapter five
Tap dancing on the wireless

After the war, play and entertainment gradually became more interesting. After school, there were a few other boys I could play with, some older and some younger, but only David Atkins and Pat Robbins were the same age as me. However, we all managed to mix together for games, although they were scattered all around the village and we had to arrange to meet up. David lived above a stable at the Court - his parents worked there. Pat Robbins lived with the Redding family on the main road. He was often called Pat Redding in error but his parents lived in Rhodesia and he had been sent back to the UK for his schooling.

There were five main places where we could play. The nearest to me was in Sumner's field, just across the road from our house. There was a large oak tree between the field and a damson orchard which we could sit beneath and across the field there was a tall pear tree in the hedge from which we could get pears in season by throwing sticks up the tree – the farmer never wanted the pears himself.

Another place was Coughton Ford, down Coughton Fields Lane at the river, where we could play on the bridge and on the rough ground around the ford. The ford was originally quite difficult for cars and one lorry became stuck and had to be abandoned near the bridge where it had ended up, but later a roadway was built straight across the river, with posts alongside measuring the depth of the water and this made it much safer except in flood conditions. We could sometimes see a car drive through the ford and those with bikes could ride around across the bridge and through the ford.

Then there was Parkes' field, which was at the bottom of our back garden and stretched from the railway line down to his apple orchard, from where we could scrump apples in season, although Len Parkes would sometimes chase us away. Caine Brook was another favourite, where we could fish for minnows, sticklebacks and red soldiers, using jam jars tied to a piece of string. There was watercress growing at the stream and we could take some home for sandwiches. Finally, there was the field behind the Throckmorton Arms, between the pub and Caine Brook. Also near the pub was a large pond which would freeze during winter and some of the older boys would run or skate across the ice, but that was too dangerous for most of us.

At one point, I don't know exactly when, I became very ill. It lasted for many weeks and the doctor had no idea what it was. I would not eat and only wanted to stay in bed. When Mum could get a couple of lemons she would make a lemon drink with sugar and water and that was the only thing I would take in. The family were very worried, thinking that I might be suffering from the same disease as my Auntie Flo.

She was my Dad's sister and she had had what they then called sleeping sickness when she was quite young and this developed into what we now know as Parkinson's disease, which was so severe that she was completely paralysed. She was looked after by her sister Ethel Bint, married to Ben and with one child Sylvia, and they lived at Littlewood Green, Studley, a few houses from Granny Lane.

We used to take Flo into our house for a few weeks sometimes to give Ethel a break. As well as being paralysed, Flo's hands shook terribly and she could only speak with difficulty. She liked me to sing her songs from the Boy Scout's songbook, and that made her laugh. I slowly recovered, however, and returned to normal with no lasting problem.

In Sumner's field, we would play cricket in the summer and football in the winter. Once we set up a course there for cycle speedway and those with bikes formed a team called Coughton Diamonds. Motorcycle speedway was very popular at the time and I once went to see it in Birmingham. There were several cycle speedway teams in the villages, notably Studley Tigers on a patch at Littlewood Green, and we made one up in Sumner's field. The Studley riders had special speedway bikes and were much faster than our team, who only had ordinary bikes, so we soon gave up. We would often play little games under the oak tree which some of the girls could join in.

In May 1946 we received some terrible news. Rob, who was serving in the Parachute Regiment in Malaya was, with 257 others, to be court-martialed for mutiny, for which the maximum penalty was death by firing squad. It was in all the papers and on the wireless news. After serving in Batavia (Indonesia) disarming the Japanese and restoring law and order, his brigade was sent to Muar in Malaya where they were camped under leaking tents in torrential rainfalls. The camp had no facilities for washing, feeding or cooking, they were living under ankle-high water, yet they were expected to parade every morning washed and shaved and in full clean uniform. The 258 had gone on strike, sitting on the seawall and refusing to go on parade. The result of the court-martial was that Rob, who was one of the eight ringleaders, was sentenced to five years penal servitude and discharged from the army "with ignominy". The others of the eight received the same and the rest were given two years hard-labour. They were all imprisoned in Kluang jail, where the Japanese had held allied prisoners of war not long before. This caused an uproar in Parliament and throughout the country. A petition was made to reverse the decision. Iris went around asking people to sign the petition and she was upset when some people refused to sign. However, half a million signatures were sent to Parliament and the court-martial result was quashed. Afterwards, after their release, we saw Rob's photo among others in the News of the World Sunday newspaper – we could hardly recognise him, he looked so thin – but we were all very relieved. After that Rob served in Palestine and after being demobbed he returned to work as a toolmaker at the Maudslay.

For several weeks there was great excitement when piped water was brought to Coughton, down the main road from Studley and then up Coughton Lane. This involved a large digging machine which dug out a channel about eighteen inches wide and three feet deep. It moved along at about 20 feet a day. I would watch it in wonder after school, checking how far it had gone each day. At the end of it, we had piped water, so Mum no longer had to carry buckets of water from the pump.

In Parkes' field, one of the elm trees had low branches which we could climb on and swing around but when the new council houses were built there the trees were cut down and easy access to the field was lost.

We played similar games behind the pub. Then every year on Boxing Day the men of the surrounding towns and villages would play a game of motorcycle football there, which was always great excitement for us as well as the players.

Sometimes a small fair would set up there once a year, but it was only one small roundabout, a couple of swinging boats and a few stalls, although some people added to it with a tug-of-war. One year a fancy dress contest was part of it and Mum, who loved these things, dressed me up as a bridegroom and Jimmy McCalman, who was a few years younger than me, as the bride. We won first prize and photos were taken of us, which for years were very embarrassing for me and I guess even more so for poor Jimmy.

During harvest time every summer I would enjoy riding on a tractor with Mr Twinberrow as he went through Cadbury's cornfields, cutting the corn. Often rabbits would run out of the corn to escape the tractor and I would jump off the tractor and try to catch them, but of course, they were far too quick.

Bonfire Night on November 5th was always much fun. We kids could only afford about ten fireworks each at the most but Peter Perkins would always invite us to his house for the bonfire as he had a hundred fireworks, so the rest of us went there with our few fireworks to add. He had a bonfire but never did he have any fireworks at all, but we fell for it every year. Peter later became a policeman.

Every year in the autumn the Mop fair would arrive and spend a couple of days at Alcester high street, then at a field at Studley and finally the big one in the main streets of Stratford. Alcester was the nearest and quite a good one. Sometimes a circus would turn up in Alcester on the playing field.

Then there were the picture houses, the Regent in Alcester, the little Cosy at Studley, and the Danilo, Gaumont and Select at Redditch.

Vic Redding would occasionally hire a coach to take people to Dudley Hippodrome to see variety shows and at Christmas to Birmingham Hippodrome to see the pantomime. I loved the variety shows and would go on the coach on my own. I was only about ten, so I guess Mum would get some of the other villagers to keep an eye on me. I think she stayed awake until I arrived home, which could be very late.

I saw comedians like Arthur Askey and double turns like Collinson and Brean and Jimmy Jewell and Ben Warriss, the forerunners of Morecombe and Wise, and a drag act called Old Mother Riley. I used to roar with laughter at the comics and the audience would often find my laughter more amusing than the acts. I found the numerous juggling acts very clever but rather boring. The singers often included a white man called G. H. Elliot who blacked up and called himself "The Chocolate-Coloured Coon", who was very popular, dressed in tropical clothes and waving a Panama hat above his head, and no-one thought there was anything wrong with what he called himself. His most famous song was "Lily of Laguna", which he always ended with, and I once read that inside his hat were the words of "Lily of Laguna" just in case he forgot them, even though he sang the song every day of his working life. Other singers included the duo of Anne Ziegler and Webster Booth.

I did not care so much for pantomimes. The only thing I can remember was that the principal boy (always played by a girl) at Birmingham every year was an actress called Hy Hazel, who had amazing legs. The coach journey to both Dudley and Birmingham had to go up Gorcott Hill and during icy weather, there was always the fear that the coach would not be able to get up Gorcott Hill, but I don't remember it ever failing to do so. Today driving along the same (re-built) road you would hardly notice a hill was there at all.

Coughton also provided some entertainment of its own at the school, which was used as a village hall in the evenings. Sometimes shows would be put on by Des and Kit Mason, either comic plays like "Box and Cox" or variety shows where everyone did their "turn". They always ended by singing "There's No Business Like Show Business", which brought a lot of sneering giggles among the audience. Much more professional were the Gilbert and Sullivan musicals performed by the Studley Operatic Society in the Entaco Hall.

Dances were also common at the school, set up by Mrs Moizer, with either a small band or a single pianist providing the music. I was too young to do much dancing but I liked the music, often sitting next to the pianist or the drummer. One violinist called George Gardner would always waltz around during the last waltz while playing his violin. The rest of our family would also be there. Mrs Moizer's son David would come in his army officer's uniform and he would only dance with Iris. Mrs Moizer was not very pleased with this, since the Moizers were considered upper class, and David stopped coming after a while. Iris was not concerned though. Sometimes fancy dress was worn, which Mum loved and would dress herself and me up, often winning a prize.

Sometimes a 'social' would be held at the school, which included dances and party games and at one of these a guest of honour was our local MP John Profumo, who came with a lady called the Duchess of Rutland. One game was a trombone playing competition, which I joined in. I came second; the winner was a lady who could play proper bugles very well. I could only blow a single note but I kept going for a long time and, afterwards, Mr Profumo told me he had been worried that I might have blown a blood vessel. Later, in 1963, Profumo had to resign following a scandalous affair with Christine Keeler.

Similar dances took place at the church hall at Sambourne and we would hire a taxi to take us there and back. Dances were a mixture of "modern" quicksteps and waltzes and "old-time" dances like the Military Two-Step, the St Bernard's Waltz and the Veleta. Other favourites were a group dance called "The Lancers", a dance in lines called the Palais Glide, a dance where partners kept changing called the Paul Jones and of course the Hokey Cokey. Rob and Clive preferred to go to the weekly dances at Alcester and Studley which were more sophisticated and where there was a much bigger choice of girl partners.

All the above entertainments were irregular and most of our enjoyment in the evenings was from the wireless. Comedy was the most popular. The first one I can remember, early in the war, was "Happydrome". There was a popular song which went "We three, we're all alone, living in a memory - my echo, my shadow and me" and Happydrome always started with a parody of this which went "We three in Happydrome, working for the BBC - Ramsbottom and Enoch and me." I don't know who the "Me" was but Enoch always did a tap dance to music. All we could hear was the music and a clickety-clack noise, which could have been anything, but people took it seriously. "Did you hear Enoch's tap dance last night? Isn't he an amazing dancer?" they would say.

Later in the war came comedy shows with a wartime theme. ITMA (It's That Man Again) was the favourite, with Tommy Handley, filled with each character producing the same comic catch-phrase each week. Then there was "Much Binding in the Marsh", making fun out of one of the many small air bases all over the country, with Richard Murdoch, Kenneth Horne and Sam Costa.

After the war, Tommy Handley died suddenly, which was a great shock to us all. The wartime shows were replaced by new ones like "Life With the Lyons", "Ray's a Laugh" and "Educating Archie". "Archie" was ventriloquist Peter Brough's dummy, but no-one thought this was strange at the time yet it was almost as weird as Enoch tap dancing on the radio.

Later still the Goon Show was one of my favourites, but the older members of my family did not see the funny side of it. We all liked Tony Hancock in "Hancock's Half Hour".

There was music too. There were many big bands like Victor Sylvester, Geraldo, Henry Hall, Joe Loss and Jack Payne (who Mum called Jack Agony). The singers included Donald Peers (Mum's favourite), Bing Crosby and the duo Anne Ziegler and Webster Booth. Another duo was Ted and Barbara Andrews, who would sometimes bring along their little daughter Julie to join in – Julie would much later become much more famous in "The Sound of Music" and other films.

Soon after the war ended Mum and Dad took me on holiday to visit my Uncle Bob and his wife in North Wales. The journey took us all day. We took the bus to Birmingham then got on the slow train to Machynlleth, calling at every little station on the way, then by bus which was going to Corris but we had to get off at Pantperthog, where my uncle lived in a detached cottage up a small inclined drive past two other cottages just off the main road to Corris. During the long train journey, Dad suggested a game we could play trying to guess the first letter of the next station. I just guessed but Dad always seemed to win by choosing the letter L every time. It was some years before I caught on to the fact that most Welsh towns and villages began with Llan, like Llandudno.

Uncle Bob worked for the Forestry Commission and had to walk many miles every day through the woods and over the mountains. His wife was a retired schoolmistress. She was rather stern, a staunch member of the Chapel and the Temperance movement. Bob liked his drink but he had to sneak off to Corris if he wanted a beer and was glad to take Dad with him for some different company.

The scenery was magnificent, looking upwards to the forests and hills and downwards to a disused miniature railway, beyond which was a river, where Dad and I went fishing for eels. The water was so clear we could watch the eels taking the bait at the bottom of the river. I had a wonderful time playing for hours at a tiny stream near the cottage, throwing sticks into it and watching them carried swiftly down the stream.

I could also ride on a miniature railway which was used to carry timber from the forest cut to size as pit props for the coal mines. It was not like a normal train engine, just a petrol-driven one on one of the small wagons, but it went miles through the woods and across many streams and I was taken sometimes by Bob but mostly by another forestry worker who was a driver and he would also take me around in his lorry to areas of interest such as Cader Idris and Tal-y-Llyn Lake.

We continued to spend holidays at Camerton. The Army had gone, Mrs Mac was back in the main part of the house and Uncle and Auntie had better servants' rooms. Joan had married Reg Power, who had been a sergeant in the Welsh Guards. He had a limp from a war wound, but that gradually disappeared, and they had a daughter Gillian. Uncle Jack was very deaf and had an early form of hearing aid, with large earphones and an amplifier which hung around his neck – he would often switch it off when he wanted some peace from all the chatter.

Both the Hudson "woody" estate car and the little red car were now in use but never the Buicks. An addition was a Ford ambulance which had been donated to the RAF in memory of her late husband by Mrs Mac and had now been returned to her. It stood unused in one of the stables but it was another for me to play in. I could also use a splendid tricycle and there were many places for me to race around with that.

The outbuilding was no longer the laundry but it was still called that and was used as a game area with table tennis, which we used quite a lot. We would usually take a day coach trip from Peasedown to either Weston-super-Mare or Weymouth and sometimes we would all go off to the dog races in Bristol, leaving me in the little red car with a bottle of lemonade and a packet of crisps until they returned.

Both Jack and Doll were characters. Jack spent most of his money at the Bristol dog races but he did wonders in the large gardens, delivering to fruit shops all over Somerset – his tomatoes were the tastiest we ever knew and he could even provide grapes and corn-on-the-cob for Mrs Mac – but he had to make sure the gardens never made a profit for tax reasons. Mrs Mac had a habit of inviting friends and relatives to dinner and only letting Doll know an hour or so beforehand, leaving her not enough time to prepare properly, so Doll set up a phone tap so that she could get early warning of visitors (and also learn other secrets too). She wired it up herself, connecting a headset to the wiring system and hiding it in an old raincoat hanging up in the hallway near her kitchen.

Mrs Mac was a gifted artist and she drew a drawing of Uncle Jack which really showed him as he was and this was framed and kept on their wall. Mrs Mac also spoke on the radio, reading novels for "Book at Bedtime" whenever an American accent was needed. She had had a tragic life. Quite apart from her husband being killed in an air crash, when she was a child in America their house was burned to the ground and while Mrs Mac escaped her mother died in the flames.

Mrs Mac once held a grand ball at Camerton – a "coming-in ball" for her niece. We were on holiday there at the time and Gillian and I acted as ushers - welcomers to the many visitors - but we had to leave before it got going.

Mrs Mac gave me an old tin full of coins which had been saved up by her husband. Some were very large religious ones, some were tokens given out by firms to their workers and a couple were gold. There was quite a selection of various sorts. I took it home and showed them to my friends. One of the older boys persuaded me to bury some underground like buried treasure, which seemed an exciting thing to do, but when I went to look at them the next day they had all gone. Another persuaded me to do the same thing, leaving them up a tree, but again they had disappeared by the next day. I was learning some of the facts of life, but very slowly.

Later, as Rob and Clive married and moved to houses of their own, we four left could eventually spend a week each year at Bournemouth, always at Chislehurst Grange, which then was run by a single man and one boy helper but is now much bigger and quite an expensive place to go.

Chapter six
Skating on thin ice

I began my studies at Alcester Grammar School in September 1949.

The school was on the outskirts of the town on the A435 Birmingham Road and I travelled the two miles on the special R15 Midland Red bus for grammar school children between Redditch and Alcester. It cost two pence each way. I had school dinner in the school canteen for six pence a day. The education was free.

Occasionally, while I waited for the bus, a large Austin 16 car would stop and the driver, who I did not know, would ask me if I wanted a lift to school. I always accepted it and was thrilled to ride in such a posh car. I told Mum about it and she said: "Oh, what a nice man!" Nowadays a mother would be horrified at such a happening, but those were safe and innocent days, in Coughton at least.

Once Mr and Mrs Moizer gave me a lift in their pre-war Rolls Royce. That was the poshest car of all and the interior was wonderful but their Rolls sounded more like a tractor than the car which prided itself that the only sound to be heard was the ticking of the clock. I think they must have had the engine replaced by diesel for economy purposes.

The headmaster of the Grammar School was a Mr Ackland for the first 18 months and afterwards was Mr Davison.

Mr Davison took the older pupils for mathematics as the time for O levels drew near. He showed no sense of humour whatsoever and regarded any joke or fun as "nonsense". Nonsense was his favourite word.

All the teachers were experts in their fields but about half of them were quite eccentric in their different ways.

I was a member of the A class in our year, there was also a B class, with 30 pupils in each class. Our first form teacher was a Miss Jolly, who taught biology and joined the school the same day as ourselves. She was aptly named, being young and vivacious, and she fancied the history teacher, Mr Lord, rather openly, but I don't think he responded in kind. She did not stay long and left the school before I did. We later heard that she was married, but not to Mr Lord.

Mr Lord was rather severe. On our first day, he gave us homework. Most of us had never heard of homework before. We didn't know what to do and so we did nothing. Next day Mr Lord went berserk and gave us twice as much to do the next day. We quickly learned the seriousness of homework.

Miss Webley was the senior mistress and she taught us English. She was very hard on the girls, even giving detention to a girl who was seen going home half a mile away walking around in her school uniform but without wearing her beret. Miss Webley had no time for those who showed any sign of humility. She called it false modesty and urged us to stand up for ourselves and outwardly show off our abilities. Fortunately, she did not bother we boys much.

Mr Druller was German and taught Latin. He also was severe and once he watched me doing some writing in class which he had given us to do, then suddenly gave me a huge slap across my ear, which knocked me sideways. I never knew what it was for and he said nothing. But, I thought at the time, he was a German and this was only five years after the war so what did I expect? I saw no purpose for Latin and gave it up as soon as I had a chance.

Mr Thornton was the chemistry teacher and his son, Anthony, who had also been at Coughton school with me, was also in our class. Mr Thornton had a very sarcastic sense of humour and could be quite unkind to some, which embarrassed his son. He also took us for sports, which meant football in the winter and cricket in the summer.

Miss Morris taught us French, she was young and tall and attractive. She once tried to explain to me that split infinitives were not a good thing (this was one time when she took us in English, not during one of her French lessons) but I couldn't get it. I could not see why infinitives should not be split if it made sense to conveniently do so.

My favourite teacher was Mr Bell, who taught us physics and mathematics. He could always sense when someone did not understand something and would give a different explanation, and even a third or fourth, until he was sure they understood. I think his accent was

Yorkshire and he would often say "Do ye understand? Dawnt say yes if ye mean naw." Years later when I became a lecturer myself I copied his methods and they put me in good stead. Mr Bell could also play ragtime on the piano, which impressed me no end. He was friendly with my brother Rob and they would play dominoes together at the Railway Inn at Studley, near where they both lived.

Miss Evans also taught mathematics. She was near retirement age and she was sometimes tongue-tied and her memory was not too good. We made fun of her but, looking back, I guess the poor woman was suffering the onset of Alzheimer's disease, although there was no such name for it at that time.

Mr Petherbridge taught us geography. His wife also taught at the school but she never taught me and I think she taught biology. They were a very nice couple and the most normal of all the teachers. Mr P was slightly dark-skinned and was nicknamed Pedro. Once he pulled me aside and gave me a warning: "You're skating on thin ice, Lancaster," he said. I don't remember what it was about but I was a bit cheeky and did not always give our teachers the respect they thought they deserved.

Mr Hadwen taught physics as well as Mr Bell but he was a Methodist minister so he was given the job of teaching scripture too. For a Christian minister, he was not a good example to us, telling us that the Bible was rubbish and giving us what amounted to indoctrination in communism. In those days it was not uncommon for some people to declare themselves openly as communist and the leader of my department at university was also a prominent communist. Mrs Hadwen was also a teacher, but not at the grammar school. She had sometimes taken over at Coughton school when Mrs Moizer was off sick and she was a very nice lady.

Each week boys would go off to Mr Moizer's woodwork school nearer the centre of Alcester while the girls took domestic science with his daughter, Margaret Moizer, at the grammar school itself. I did not learn much about woodwork – we were just given a piece of wood and told to get on with something while Mr Moizer went on with building his boat. I did make a pair of bookends which were very plain and I ended up trying to make a wooden sextant but never finished it. Mr Moizer's boat was so big that he had to remove the windows to enable it to be carried out after he had finished it. I sometimes thought I would rather have done domestic science because Margaret Moizer was very glamorous.

Teachers of music and art came and went very frequently and I don't remember much about the teachers or the subjects. One male music teacher came to school driving a 1920s vintage Delage open-top roadster, a monster of a car and very noisy, but he only lasted a year at most.

I did very well at the grammar school, being second in the class for the first year and usually third for the remainder. Head of the class was always Ann Swinglehurst. She was the daughter of a local garage owner in Alcester and no-one in the class could ever beat her. She seemed too good to be true, able to play the piano perfectly to music seemingly without effort, good at all sports and very beautiful, with long black plaits. She was always going to leave the rest of us behind.

The one thing I hated at school was sports and physical education. Iris once asked mum why I was being so grumpy one day as I prepared to go. "Oh, it's sport today," she replied as I stuffed my bag with my sports clothes and boots. Mr Thornton chose a few of the keener types to be leaders and they tended to dominate.

I was always left-back at soccer, always on the outfield during cricket and last to bat. One day, during football, all the play was at the other end of the field and myself and the goalkeeper became bored and started throwing bits of dirt at each other. Suddenly we realized that all play had stopped and Mr Thornton and all the other players were staring at us and giggling. It didn't embarrass me, I thought sport was a lot of nonsense, as Mr Davison would have put it. I think it was because I could never accept the idea of teamwork. Being inherently lazy I could not understand why I should put myself out for the benefit of the other ten. Later in life, I enjoyed deck tennis when at sea and golf when ashore and then snooker after retirement, but I was never good at any of it.

Physical education was treated as a separate subject. Again we had several teachers who came and went frequently and I liked it no better. The horses we were supposed to be able to jump over in the gym were as tall as me and I was no good at anything, with the one exception of climbing up the ropes. I was very thin, there was no weight to me and I had no trouble in pulling myself quickly to the very top, touching the high ceiling, which the others seemed unable to do. Worst of all was the long-distance running. The course was partly by road and partly over the fields and about two miles. The teacher would ride his bike alongside us, shouting at us to go faster, until we entered the fields when he would ride back to the school. Then I would, together with several others, take a short cut across the railway line, which halved the total distance, but I would still be beaten by those who went the whole way.

A friend of my father's, Bert Deakin, who lived down by Caine's Brook and worked at the Royal Enfield factory in Redditch, once gave me a "blueprint" of a crystal receiver which had been given away with his copy of "Practical Wireless" magazine. This was a circuit and details of how to build a crystal receiver, which needed no battery or mains connection. I built it and was thrilled when I could hear the BBC Home Service on it. This was the start of my interest in the workings of radio equipment. (Later in life I was to write several series of articles for Practical Wireless). Bert later gave me an old radio which he had replaced and Philip Caile lent me a short wave receiver and gave me lots of bits and pieces of electrical components and encouraged me by showing me things he had done, which even included a television receiver with a tiny green screen and made from old wartime radar equipment.

I pored over copies of "Practical Wireless" ("Wireless World" was too difficult), built some simple receivers and attended the local Radio Amateur's Club in Redditch as a "short-wave listener". There were lots of components for radio receivers available from shops which sold ex-wartime items and Iris gave me money to buy some. I built a short wave radio with which I could listen to radio stations from all over the world – the man from Studley Radio shop made the aluminium frame for it. I would record (on paper) amateur radio stations and send them my "short-wave radio listener" card and they would send me their card in return. I won a prize at the school sports day exhibition when I exhibited the radio and all the cards I had received.

On Sundays, for a year or two, I served on the altar at Coughton Parish Church whenever the vicar did holy communion. It was not that I was in any way religious but I regarded the church as a tradition which showed us the difference between right and wrong, the Harrisons were good people and I just wanted to help them. I would have to wait another thirty or more years before I became a committed Christian.

The Rev Harrison had been a padre in the Royal Navy during the war. He heard of my interest in radio and suggested I might like a career as a ship's radio officer in the Merchant Navy. Living in a small village in rural Warwickshire, just about as far from the sea as you can get on our island, I had never heard of such an occupation and neither had the occupation adviser who visited the school (I had to tell him all about it). So the vicar sent off for a copy of Marconi's recruitment brochure and presented it to me. I still have it today. It shows two pictures of the same youth on the front - one wearing a school cap and the other a naval officer's cap. It describes this magical career of travelling around the world on ships of all types, operating and maintaining radio equipment and being paid for it as well. From that day on I never once considered any other career and I must have read that brochure thousands of times. I would gaze out of our front window over the lawn and pretend I was looking out to sea from the bridge window of a ship.

On Friday afternoons at school, we could join one of the many clubs available. At first, I joined the Boy Scouts and got all the equipment for it, but I soon found out it was not for me. I then joined the radio club, but I was the only member and spent every other Friday afternoon for the rest of my schooldays building bits of radio gear, looked over by Mr Hadwen. My fellow pupils thought I was obsessed (and they were probably right) and they nicknamed me Marconi.

Several of my fellow boy pupils later joined the police force after they had done their National Service.

One year a school outing to France was on offer for our year. We were given all the details to take home for our parents to see and we had to say whether we would go or not. I knew my parents would not be able to afford it so I did not even tell them about it. I would soon be travelling much farther than France anyway so I did not feel I was missing anything special.

Much more exciting to me was when I was taken to see the 1954 International Trophy Race at Silverstone.

My friend Clive Oseland, whose father ran a newspaper shop at Stratford, invited me to join them. I cycled the ten miles to Stratford and back and was taken in Mr Oseland's big Morris car. We watched the race won by Jose Froilan Gonzalez in a Ferrari. Unfortunately, British Grand Prix cars were going through losing times but a new Lagonda was expected to be a sensation in the sports car race, but only managed to come fifth. But it was all such a thrill and I have never forgotten it.

I could not wait to leave school when I was sixteen and go to college. Mr Davison heard about it and thought it was all nonsense - he wanted me to stay on into the sixth form and go to university, but I was having none of that. Although I had done well at the Grammar School, I felt that I was reaching my peak. The other pupils were catching up with me and some overtaking me. Also, I sat in on one of Mr Davison's lessons to the sixth formers and I did not like what I heard. I could cope with sines, cosines and tangents but cot, sec and cosec, together with calculus, seemed to be taking mathematics too far for my liking and it all seemed irrelevant to what I wanted to do. I was surprised Mr Davison couldn't see that it was a lot of nonsense.

I did complete my O level exams and passed all eight, which was the maximum we were allowed to take. There were only two grades in those days – pass or fail.

Before I left the Grammar School, Dad bought me an ex-wartime 125cc Royal Enfield motorcycle from Bert Deakin, who had had it fully reconditioned and it was like new. It had been built for paratroopers to use after they had landed, so it was light enough to be parachuted itself. It had a hand-change gear lever and could only do 30 mph maximum but I thought it was wonderful. I rode it to school one day but Mr Davison soon told me not to bring such nonsense to school again. It was the start of new enthusiasm for me with motorbikes and I loved riding it around the villages but I soon longed for one more powerful and faster.

One lad in Coughton Lane had a Douglas Dragonfly, which I thought was wonderful, and Clive's friend Geoff Caile had a Triumph Speed Twin and later a Scott Flying Squirrel and both of these were beyond the wildest dreams of both myself and Clive and Rob, who had their own pre-war BSAs and Royal Enfields. Most days a pair of test riders tested new Sunbeam bikes from Redditch - they seemed to test every new bike from Redditch to Coughton and back, turning at the crossroads. I spent many Saturdays going to motorcycle grass track races at Astwood Bank and later dirt track races just off the Worcester Road beyond Inkberrow.

My Dad was thrilled that I might one day become an **officer** - men in our immediate family had only ever served as "other ranks" in the army - but he would never be able to afford to keep me at college for a year. So he went cap-in-hand (he always wore a cloth cap with a button on the top) to our local county council representative, with me in tow, and pleaded for a grant. It worked, and I was given £180 to go to Southampton University for a year to study for the basic certificate which would allow me to go to sea as a radio officer.

Again the education was free, the money was for living in lodgings. That was even more than I had hoped for and I could even afford to run my motorbike on it. I started the course in September 1954.

Chapter seven
Dances at the
swear house

After I started at the Grammar School in 1949 I still went out to play after school with the other boys and some girls around the village before doing my homework later on.

For one period, we played outside the pub and I became friendly with a girl called Jean, who lived at the top of the hill on the main road. We began going cycle rides together, so I guess she was my first girlfriend, or at least a friend who happened to be a girl. She became very ill and I went to see her as she lay in bed but soon afterwards I fell out with other members of the group and didn't see Jean again.

In 1951, Iris took me to see the Festival of Britain in London, where we stayed with Uncle Jack. The Festival was a big thing at the time, showing lots of new scientific developments. The fairgrounds at Battersea Park were thrilling, with a roller-coaster passing through tunnels, the "wall of death", motorboats around the pond and lots more – much better than Alcester Mop and ten times more expensive. We also visited the British Museum and in the evening went to a show to see Leslie Hutchinson (Hutch), a famous black pianist and singer, at the Empire, Finsbury Park (not quite the West End).

On Saturday afternoons there was cricket. The cricket field was just north of Caine Brook and it had a pavilion, although this was in a rather shabby state. I was too young to be part of the team but I noted down all the scores and later posted details to the local newspaper, the Redditch Indicator, which filled up a few spaces for them. Mum and Iris helped with the tea and sandwiches. Dad liked to see it but he was getting a bit too old to play, although he did do so sometimes if any team was short of a player.

Mum and I began going to whist drives, some at Sambourne church hall and some at Cookhill school. At Cookhill I met a girl called Rosemary and built up enough courage to ask her to meet me separately. She had a horse and would ride down to Coughton to meet me. I was 15 at the time and I think she was younger so it was not much of a romance. I don't think we even kissed and I cannot imagine what we found to talk about. It ended very suddenly when I caught the shingles. I can remember exactly when it was since I was in bed suffering when Queen Elizabeth's coronation took place on the second of June 1953. Everyone around went to the Boots' house to watch it on TV because they were the only ones in the street who had a set. I missed that altogether and I was not able to contact Rosemary to let her know why I didn't meet her so it ended there (no-one we knew had telephones, except Camerton Court).

Mum, Iris and I tried to get Dad to agree to buy a TV set but he would not have it for years. Mr and Mrs Lippett, who lived at the junction of the main road and Sambourne Lane, opposite the old blacksmith's forge, were the first people we knew to have a TV and they said I could go and watch it with them any time. I took full advantage of their offer and might have outstayed my welcome but their two daughters had both married and left the family home and they seemed happy to have me there for company.

The TV had a 12-inch screen and had to be seen in utter darkness, otherwise, it would not be bright enough, and the picture was obliterated by interference every time a car passed by (this only stopped when cars had to be fitted with high resistance plug leads). There was only one programme – the BBC – which came on twice a day – once in the afternoon and again in the evening, so I spent many evenings with the Lippetts for a while.

I gradually became more interested in girls and the main way of meeting members of the opposite sex in those days was to go to a dance, where a boy could ask any girl to dance, which enabled them to be close together and to chat. The girls did not have the same choice, it being bad manners for them to refuse to dance with any boy who asked them, although there might be one "ladies invitation" dance where they could choose for themselves. I learned to dance waltzes and quicksteps well enough to get by and these were the main dances. For foxtrots, I would do a slower quickstep which many people did. There was the occasional tango, rhumba or samba, but very few of these as they were only for the more serious dancers.

The two main places for me to go on Saturday nights were the Alcester Town Hall (which Mum had told me was the Swear House) in an upstairs room and Studley Entaco Hall. There were two main bands, the Quavers and the Night Hawks, the latter being slightly jazzier than the Quavers. If I didn't fancy any of the girls at Alcester I would ride off on my bike to Studley.

I was very young at 15 to go dancing but Mum and Dad seemed quite happy for me to go, although I'm sure Mum did not go to sleep until she heard me come back home after midnight. Most girls were older than me, of course, but there were a few of my age. None of the Grammar School girls of my age ever came but there were some from the National School.

Looking down from the upstairs dances at Alcester Town Hall I could see Ann Swinglehurst's house and I wished she would come but she never did and I never asked her. I did go out with her once to the Mop and we had a good time. Afterwards, she invited me back to her house to meet her mother, who, after chatting for a while, suggested we play a card game. I had played cards with our family and their friends the Blakes but the game we played here was Canasta, which involved two decks of cards and was very complicated compared to all the other games I had played. I could not understand what I was supposed to do and made a complete mess of it. I had the impression that I was being tested to see if I was intelligent enough for her daughter's attention and felt embarrassed by it all.

Looking back I think her mother was just being sociable and I was being super-sensitive but I didn't ask Ann out again and she didn't seem to take any further interest in me.

I once took tango lessons run by a pair of dancing instructors in Redditch. I was the youngest male there and took a fancy to one girl who was probably in her early twenties. I chose her to dance with at every opportunity, which embarrassed her and amused her friends. I knew I was embarrassing her but I did not care, but after a while, I became ashamed of what I was doing and stopped going.

The girls from the other school were looking for boyfriends so it was easier for me to get to know them. It was usual for a boy to ask a girl if he could take her home after the dance ended. The older girls would expect this to be by car or motorcycle and I would be embarrassed to have to put on my bicycle clips after the dance to cycle the 2 miles back to Coughton, but the younger girls did not expect anything more.

Taking a girl home, of course, was just an excuse to get closer and would involve kissing and possibly heavy petting, but some girls wanted sex. There was no contraceptive pill in those days and any contraceptives available were crude and unreliable. It was normal in those days if a girl became pregnant for the boy to feel bound to marry her. Unmarried mothers were left in a very bad position, disgraced and perhaps having to let their child be adopted and lost forever – there was not normally any possibility of having an abortion - so most girls would not agree to have full sex. Boys were often just as fearful of having to marry someone they did not love. For myself, it would also have meant that I would not feel able to go to sea in the Merchant Navy, which I wanted more than anything, and I often felt I was more fearful of having sex than the girls were of becoming pregnant.

The one exception to my fears was Jill, a pretty fair-haired girl. She was much taller than me, which was not perfect for a dancing partner, but she had a beautiful voice, sometimes singing along with the dance band. I would walk her home after the dance and we would kiss outside her house, with her looking down on me. By this time I was 16 and was tempted, but she was sensible and resisted my advances, which was just as well since I found out many years later that while I was 16 she was only 14. Instead of going to sea, I could have ended up going to gaol. Our courtship ended when I had to study for my O levels and then go off to college. I did not think any girl would want a boyfriend who spent ten months a year swanning off around the world.

Chapter eight
The road to poverty and ostentation

I started the one-year course for Second Class PMG at Southampton University in September 1954. This was the Postmaster General's Certificate, which enabled people to serve as radio officers in the British Merchant Navy. At that time everything that involved wireless communications (radio) was controlled by the General Post Office in the UK, which was based in London.

The course was not a degree course. It had been run at Southampton Polytechnic but this had just become a university and the course was continued there for a few years afterwards. So I was at university but not doing a degree course and those like me were naturally looked down on by those taking degree courses. However, we were allowed to take advantage of all the same things as degree students, which involved using the refectory both for meals and evening entertainment.

Not being on a degree course meant that I could not live in the university accommodation but had to find lodgings. I found a room in a large old house in the Saint Denys area of the city. Three other students were living there as well, two doing the same course as myself and a Pakistani lad who was doing a degree course.

Our landlady was a Mrs Smith, an elderly widow who had once run a hotel in Dorchester with her husband and four sons, so her dinners were excellent. I thought I would miss my favourite radio programmes so I hired a large radio from Radio Rentals but I soon discovered that I had too many new interests to be bothered with the wireless any more. Mrs Smith treated us like her own sons, keeping us on the straight and narrow, but I'm afraid we teased her and made fun of her until we discovered that all four of her sons had been killed fighting during the war. I never met any other person who had suffered so much from the effects of war and we made sure we were much kinder to her from then on.

On Wednesday and Saturday evenings I went to dances. There were plenty of choices. The Guildhall was the largest venue, then there was the Marlands Hall nearby and the Ordnance Survey offices which used their canteen on those evenings. There were also dances at the end of the pier but they were notorious for fights, being used by the local Teddy-boys, so I did not go there. I did now have my motorbike, which helped in finding girlfriends, and I went out with a few I met at the dances, mostly to the cinema or music shows, but none of them lasted very long once they found out I was about to go off to sea. One girl was the daughter of the Chief Steward of one of the Cunard Queens and he was more adamant than most that I was not suitable for his daughter.

Once a week there was traditional jazz in the University Refectory and I began a lifelong love of that kind of jazz and blues, which was very popular at the time. We had some very good bands there, even Humphrey Lyttleton, who was one of the very best and who I went to hear at Winchester one evening as well. I bought a gramophone and some long-playing jazz records, also a cornet, followed by a clarinet. However, after a few days of trying each of these instruments, I felt I would never be any good at either and soon got rid of them. (When I told Dad I had paid thirty shillings (£1.50) for one record he laughed and thought I was joking since he had only known 78 records at about sixpence each).

The technical work on my course was part theory and part practical, the practical being fault-finding on the marine radio equipment. The lecturer would deliberately put faults on a piece of equipment and we would have to find out what was wrong and fix it. This was part of the final examination. All the equipment in those days was analogue and used high voltages. Once I was working on a direction finder and suffered a severe electric shock from 250 volts which temporarily caused two fingers in my right hand to lock up – it was a close thing and I was extremely careful after that.

I found the technical work easy because I was so keen, but the morse code was a different matter. We spent all our afternoons supposedly practising our morse, but it was so boring that we often persuaded our lecturer to spin us yarns about his time in the Royal Navy for most of this time. As a result, I passed the technical papers and practical tests easily but failed the morse and had to go up to London for a retest at GPO headquarters. I passed this, undeservedly I must confess, but I think there was such a shortage of Radio Officers at the time that I was nodded through.

We students used to chat about going to sea and which company we would like to work for when the time came and we would quiz the lecturers. There were three main companies which employed radio officers and would rent them out to shipping companies – these were Marconi Marine, International Marine Radio and Siemens Brothers. Some shipping companies employed their radio officers directly.

I once saw the P & O liner *Iberia* arriving at the docks and was very impressed. P & O (the Peninsular and Oriental Steam Navigation Company) employed their radio officers directly so I decided I would seek employment with them when the time came. When I mentioned this to the lecturers they were very dismissive about that company, saying that P & O employees had to put up with a lot of "bull" and one of them said that P & O stood for "Poverty and Ostentation". However, I did eventually join that company and never regretted it.

As part of our education, we were taken on board the Union-Castle liner *Pretoria Castle*, which was in dock, to visit the radio office and have a general look around the ship. It was interesting and this company employed their own radio officers, but their ships only went to South Africa and I was hoping for something a bit more adventurous.

At the end of my first year, when I had passed the Second Class PMG certificate and was therefore qualified to serve in the Merchant Navy, Warwickshire County Council offered to increase my grant to £220 a year if I would stay on for another two terms to get my First Class PMG certificate and Radar Maintenance certificate, which I accepted gratefully.

Mrs Smith told us she was not well enough now to carry on keeping lodgers so I had to find new lodgings. I stayed in two places in the Portswood area before ending up at 46 Mayfield Road, very close to the university. I went to visit Mrs Smith once. She was now very ill and had a nurse with her when I visited. Soon afterwards I passed her house and saw it was being demolished, so I assumed the poor lady had died or gone to a home.

During the long summer holidays from Southampton University, I found a job so that I could save up some spending money for my return.

The first job in 1954 was driver's mate on a lorry which took cardboard packs of orange juice from a farm in Sambourne to districts some miles away, as far as Wales. It was very easy, just sitting in the cab most of the time and helping the driver load and unload the packs as necessary. The lady who ran the business had a very flashy car – an Austin Atlantic drophead coupe. The only excitement was in Wales when the driver turned onto a pavement where we were about to unload and the paving slabs broke up under the weight. There was much anger and threats of prosecution but we drove off amid it all and I don't think anything else came from it.

The next year was more interesting. We had a couple of very good friends, Mr and Mrs Blake, who lived at Harvington, between Alcester and Evesham. Mr Blake was the foreman on a large farm there and he got me a job driving a small Ferguson tractor.

The first job was to pull a cutting machine through a field of cabbages and cut them all to pieces. The price of cabbages had fallen to the point where it was not worth sending them to market. I thought it such a waste after all the years of hunger and I took several cabbages home. Mum had made some cheese sandwiches for me to take in a haversack for lunch and at one point the haversack fell off the tractor and under the cutting machine and was destroyed. I thought I would have to go hungry but after a short time, the farmer's wife came along with some sandwiches. I couldn't understand how she knew because no-one was around when it happened and the farmhouse was two fields away. Later Mr Blake told me that the farmer watched over all his workers through a telescope and would have seen it happen.

Most of the time I was pulling a trailer through the orchards, picking up baskets of fruit from the pickers and taking them to the apple barn, where between ten and twenty local women sorted them out in different sizes for sending to market.

Once I was driving down a steep hill in one of the plum orchards when I found I could not stop the tractor, despite standing on the brake with all my might. In a panic, I turned the tractor towards a plum tree and hit it quite hard. Plums from the tree and the trailer flew everywhere and then I saw that a man had been up a ladder picking from that very tree and he came down shaking like a leaf. I think I must have been standing on the clutch as well as the brake, I could think of no other reason for it and it did not happen again.

Some of the pickers were a group of gipsies. One of these was a very glamorous girl, very slim with long black hair and quite fiery, just like the kind of gipsy girl to be seen in the movies. All the male pickers lusted after her but the gipsies kept to themselves. No one ever knew her name and I only ever heard her called "Smithy's daughter". Smith was a very common name generally but especially so among the gipsies.

When my time came to leave in September 1955 I knew I would not be back again because I would be off to sea by May the following year. On my last day, Mr Blake told me the women in the apple barn wanted me to go there to say goodbye. These women were a rather ribald lot and they had been known to capture one of the men and pull his trousers off, so I was very wary about going there. But when I entered the barn they all clapped and then sang "All the nice girls love a sailor."

Back at Southampton I was becoming frustrated with the slow speed and lack of street cred of my Enfield motorcycle so I decided to look for something more exotic. I found a Morgan three-wheeler sports car which could be driven with a motorcycle licence because it had no rear gear. It was on sale for £35 and I was only offered £7 for my bike, but I thought I could afford it. However, when I discovered that the insurance for it would cost £35 every year, that was an end of the matter. (At the time of writing such a car would cost £35,000 now).

I changed my bike for a 250cc BSA which would do 50 mph but Dad was upset that I'd changed the shining as-new bike he had bought me. Later I changed the BSA for a 350cc Matchless, which I thought would be good for 70 mph and even had telescopic front forks, but it was an ex-Army one and must have been under-geared as it still only did about 50 mph.

During the Autumn term of 1955, I took the radar course. This was on radar maintenance. Covering the technical understanding of radar and much practical fault-tracing work, I had no difficulty with this and was awarded my certificate for the Maintenance of Radar Equipment on Merchant Ships, issued by the Ministry of Transport and Civil Aviation in January 1956.

Sometime during the winter, I went off on my Matchless to Camerton where my parents and Iris were visiting. The weather was freezing and the journey back to Southampton was a nightmare. I had very thick clothes and gloves but I was still so cold I could not use my fingers to use the clutch or brakes and had to use the forks by bending my wrists around them. When I got back to my lodgings the landlady was out and I had no key with me, so I had to wait on the doorstep for a long time in the freezing cold until she eventually returned. That was the end of my love of motorbikes.

The Spring Term took me back to radio. The First Class certificate was just a more advanced version of the Second Class, involving morse at 25 words per minute instead of 20 and a more searching technical examination with a pass rate of 75%. I passed the technical theory and practical but failed the morse again, and once more I was awarded a dodgy pass after a resit. It was now April 1956 and I was ready to begin my life at sea.

No sooner had I received my first class certificate than I received a telegram from a shipping company called the Brocklebank Line, who employed their own radio officers, offering me a job, but it was P & O for me, so I applied to P & O and was granted an interview. Their head office then was at 122 Leadenhall Street and I wandered into the vast entrance hall with my mouth wide open. There were huge models of their ships in glass cases all around, with magical names like *Iberia, Arcadia, Himalaya, Chusan* and the Strath liners (*Strathmore, Stratheden, Strathnaver and Strathaird*).

I was directed to the mezzanine floor and, after discovering what a mezzanine floor was, I found myself in the office of the Radio Department. The Head of Department was the genial Commander Dennis Barnes and second-in-command was the brilliant but eccentric Philip Bendelow. Another elderly gentleman hovered silently in the background - his name was Macbeth. They seemed pleased with me but said they had no vacancies at that moment but would write to me when they had one. At that time I believed everything adults told me, so I was not at all discouraged. They advised me to go and get some sea time in while awaiting a summons from them.

I applied to International Marine Radio, had an interview at their head office in Croydon, and was appointed as third Radio Officer to the Cunard liner *Saxonia*. She was in Liverpool and as I had to be there about a week later I hastily bought my uniforms and two large fibre suitcases.

I travelled up to Liverpool the night before I was due to report on board and stayed in a run-down boarding house on Lime Street overnight. The ship was in Huskisson Dock and the next morning I took the overhead railway to get there. I wore civvies, of course, I had been told not to wear uniform ashore. What a marvellous facility this rickety little railway in the air was! It was so exciting riding high above the docks and seeing all the ships. (I did not realise it then, but the railway was closed later that year - what a shame!).

I soon ran into a problem that was going to be with me for many years. I was by then 18 years old but looked about 12. A party of schoolchildren was being ushered up the steps behind me at the station and one of the teachers ordered me to get into line with the others. It was only when he saw my two heavy suitcases that he realised his mistake. (By the way, why did it take hundreds of years for inventors to think of putting wheels onto suitcases?).

The *Saxonia* was most impressive. All 21,637 tons of her towered above the quay and she was almost new, having sailed on her maiden voyage only eighteen months previously. Up to this point, apart from that brief visit to the *Pretoria Castle* I had never actually set foot aboard a ship of any kind and felt so privileged to have this grand liner as my first.

There were two gangways. The forward one had a sign which read "Officers and Visitors Only" and the after one "Crew and Shore Staff". I struggled up the forward gangway with my cases and was met at the top by a burly fellow in uniform who I later learned was something called a quartermaster. "Who are you?" he demanded. "I'm the Third Radio Officer", I announced proudly. "And I'm Lord Nelson," he growled. "Get down the after gangway". He looked so important that I did not question this order, but struggled back down the gangway, along the quay, up the aft gangway, up and down stairs aboard the ship and along alleyways, getting lost umpteen times, and finally staggered into the radio office, where the other two Radio Officers were waiting for me.

Their faces dropped when I said who I was and that it was my first trip to sea. The chief was very elderly - long past normal retiring age. He had been persuaded (or maybe he had volunteered) to stay on because of staff shortages. The second was, I guessed, in his forties, and had a very strong Scouse accent. They soon made it clear that they did not think it right for a first-tripper like me to walk into the job on £28 a month (the starting salary had been £21 ever since the Great Depression, so I believe, until the very month I joined).

They also voiced the opinion that no R/O should be given a First Class ticket until he had completed a year's sea time. This idea was very prevalent at the time and I could see the sense of it, but I had been encouraged to do what I did and I hadn't made the rules.

The previous third had had some sea experience before joining, had been a particularly close friend of the second and the best third they had ever come across. People kept calling in at the radio office and expressing their sympathy to the second for losing his friend, who had been sent to another ship, while giving me sidelong glances. It was not the welcome I had been expecting.

I was sent back ashore to get some documents. Pool forms (I never did find out what they were for) and a discharge book are the only two I can remember. By the time I had my photo taken for my discharge book I was thoroughly fed up, having walked from office to office in the rain, and that photo has been scowling out at me from my discharge book ever since.

I had to sign on in the galley. I was amazed at the sight of the galley interior, not so much at all the equipment but that the floor was concrete! I had always thought that ships' decks were made of wooden planking. The other floors I had walked on in the ship had all been carpeted, but I had been confident that there was wooden planking underneath.

My time aboard the *Saxonia* was one of the worst experiences of my life and I wondered whether I had done the right thing. I did two voyages to Montreal and Quebec, miserable and seasick all the time, but at our second call at Quebec, I received a letter from P & O telling me that I could join them on my return. So, once back in the UK I resigned from IMR and headed straight for 122 Leadenhall Street where I re-examined the ship models. Which would be mine? The *Iberia* perhaps? That would be ideal. But they were all big white liners heading for the golden sands of India, Australia or the exotic Far East, and hopefully through calm waters.

Back on the mezzanine floor in the office with Dennis Barnes, I received a warm welcome. "What would be my first P & O ship?" I enquired. "We're sending you as fourth radio officer of the good ship *Empire Haw-weigh*", announced Dennis. To Dennis, they were all 'good ships'.

"The what?!!!" I did not speak the words but they must have been written all over my face. "The *Empire Haw-weigh*," he repeated. In P & O head office the name Fowey was always pronounced *Haw-weigh*. "She's a troopship," he explained. (She had formerly been the German liner *Potsdam*.)

"Where does she go?" I asked feebly, too dumbfounded to think of anything else to say. "The Far and Dizzy East", was the reply.

Well, that didn't sound too bad. At least I would be going somewhere which might feel abroad, unlike Montreal and Quebec.

I had to have my wavy line sleeve braiding changed to P & O gold-with-green epaulettes and had to buy a lot more other uniforms – mess kit, tropical white suits and a cummerbund, which I had never heard of before. Somehow I got them all into the same two suitcases.

I boarded the *Empire Fowey* in Southampton. As I reached the officers' accommodation around mid-day, all the noise was coming from just one cabin, so I knocked on its door, marked Third Officer, and peered inside. It was packed with officers, all much younger than their Cunard counterparts, and all quaffing gins and tonics. I said who I was and was given a very warm welcome. They wanted to know all about me. I squatted on one of my cases and had a gin thrust into my hand. The cabin was decorated with exotic oriental pictures and ornaments such as a table lamp in the shape of a Chinese lantern. This was a very different world to that of the *Saxonia*.

However, the *Fowey* took me off to war! We took troops to invade Egypt at the end of 1956. But the *Fowey* was a happy ship and after that war was over we went to Dennis's Far and Dizzy East (Singapore and Hong Kong – via South Africa because the Suez Canal was closed) then, after that voyage, I was sent to the passenger liner *Strathmore,* heading for South Africa and on to Australia, and I was at last in the real land of Poverty and Ostentation.

Also by Roger Lancaster

The Outsider's Guide To Christianity (2021)
Austin Macauley Publishers Ltd

THE REAL PRESS
www.therealpress.co.uk

if you enjoyed this book, could you please leave us a review? If makes the most enormous difference to small publishers like us – on Amazon, or Goodreads or maybe even both!

We are a very small, very independent publisher, and reviews make a huge difference to us...

You might also like either of the following:

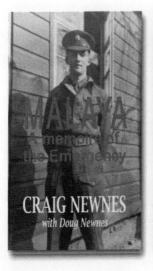